SpringerBriefs in Computer Science

For further volumes:
http://www.springer.com/series/10028

Mark L. Braunstein

Health Informatics in the Cloud

 Springer

Mark L. Braunstein
Professor of the Practice
  School of Interactive Computing
  College of Computing
Associate Director for Health Systems
  Institute for People and Technology
Georgia Institute of Technology
Atlanta, GA, USA

ISBN 978-1-4614-5628-5   ISBN 978-1-4614-5629-2 (eBook)
DOI 10.1007/978-1-4614-5629-2
Springer New York Heidelberg Dordrecht London

Library of Congress Control Number: 2012948134

Printed on acid-free paper

Springer is part of Springer Science+Business Media (www.springer.com)

To Rowena, my wife and the "real physician" in the family. She has always kept me grounded in the realities of medical practice and the healthcare system and well stocked with her world class baked goods.

Preface

This book is intended to help students and other interested readers gain basic proficiency in health[1] informatics, the application of computing to healthcare delivery, public health and community-based clinical research. This is distinct from the related field of bioinformatics, which explores the role of computing in understanding the genomic and proteomic processes within cells. I only mention this because the two are often confused.

The book is written for the non-technical reader and follows the approach I use in my Introduction to Health Informatics course at Georgia Tech. Chapters 1 and 2 discuss the US healthcare delivery system's unique structural, economic and policy issues. Chapter 3, the most technically intense, explains at a high level the core technologies involved in contemporary health informatics. Chapters 4-7 look at how these technologies are actually being deployed using some of what I consider the best commercial products as examples. Chapter 8 is my own personal speculation about the future of the field. I provide a glossary of some of the most common terms and acronyms you will encounter in the book and elsewhere should you further explore the field. I also provide some suggested reading resources at the end.

There are existing texts (*Medical Informatics* by Shortliffe, Perreault, Wiederhold, and Fagan; and *Guide to Health Informatics* by Coiera) that cover the field from a technical approach more appropriate for the informatics professional. Where possible, based on my far from perfect knowledge, I have acknowledged some of the early visionaries of the field to give the reader historical perspective. I apologize for any omissions I may have made in this regard.

You may be wondering what computing has to do with improving healthcare delivery. For the answer we'll go to the organization that, more than any other, has focused serious attention on our healthcare delivery system's problems and the role computing can help play to solve them.

---

[1] I generally use the term "health" to include both the healthcare delivery system ("healthcare") and other activities (e.g. by the patient, public health) to maintain wellness and prevent disease.

Established in 1970, the Institute of Medicine (IOM) is an independent, nonprofit organization that works outside of government to provide unbiased and authoritative advice to decision makers and the public. It is the health arm of the National Academy of Sciences, chartered under Abraham Lincoln in 1863. Starting in 2001, with the IOM's pronouncement that our health "system" [2] is neither safe, effective or efficient [1] there has been increasing recognition that information technology could and, indeed, must play the same transformative role in healthcare that it has in other industries.

In 2004 President George W. Bush pronounced a national goal of universal adoption of electronic health records and health information exchanges by 2014. How could health informatics rise to a level of importance that merits being called a national priority in the most highly visible presidential address of the year? What does it have to do with solving the problems the IOM identified? These are some of the questions we'll explore.

In 2009 President Obama used the American Recovery and Reconstruction Act (ARRA, the "Stimulus") to set aside up to $39 billion to fund adoption of electronic health records and to create health information exchanges along with a number of related programs to spur adoption and to pave the way for further development of the field. I feel it is also spawning a new wave of innovative entrepreneurial activity, most of it based in the cloud, the inspiration for the title of this book. Cloud computing has the goal of making computer resources available as they are needed somewhat like other utilities we all rely on such as electricity and water. When combined with the increasing utilization of wireless and mobile technologies it offers a truly transformative platform for healthcare delivery.

The massive ARRA funding seems to be leading to the eventual achievement of Bush's goal, although adoption will surely not be universal until a number of years after 2014. [2] However, there seems to be growing momentum. In June, 2012 the Department of Health and Human Services (HHS) said that more than 110,000 eligible professionals (around 20%) and 2,400 hospitals (nearly 50%) had received Meaningful Use incentive payments surpassing HHS' goal of 100,000 providers by the end of 2012. In July, 2012 the CDC's National Center for Health Statistics' (NCHS) 2011 survey of physician adoption [3] showed that 55% of physicians had adopted an EHR and around 75% of these said their EHR system was capable of achieving Meaningful Use. Even more positively, 85% of the adopters reported being somewhat (47%) or very (38%) satisfied with their system and 75% said that it had improved patient care.

There may be other forces for adoption. In Massachusetts by 2015, physicians must demonstrate proficiency in "computerized physician order entry, e-prescribing, electronic health records and other forms of health information technology" to maintain their licensure. [4] Medicare and the largest private health insurers are

---

[2] Hereafter, I won't put the word system in quotes when it refers to healthcare delivery in the US. I do so here to make a point – one of the central problems is that healthcare delivery in our country isn't delivered via a system if you accept most standard definitions of that term. Indeed it is a "complex adaptive system" as described by my colleague, Dr. Bill Rouse.

implementing new care models that virtually demand adoption for successful implementation.

Given these substantial changes in the nature of computing and in healthcare delivery I believe now is a particularly auspicious time for this book.

1. Committee on Quality of Healthcare in America (2001) Crossing the Quality Chasm: A New Health System for the 21st Century. The National Academies Press
2. Blumenthal D (2011) Implementation of the Federal Health Information Technology Initiative. N Engl J Med 365:2426-2431
3. Jamoom E, Beatty P *et al* (2012) Physician Adoption of Electronic Health Record Systems: United States, 2011, NCHS Data Brief, No. 98
4. http://www.malegislature.gov/Laws/GeneralLaws/PartI/TitleXVI/Chapter112/ Section2. Accessed 19 July, 2012

Atlanta, GA, USA   Mark L. Braunstein

Acknowledgments

The reviewers of the first version of this book were my physician wife and my daughter, Emily, a computer scientist. They provided wonderful, candid input and suggestions to make things clearer and to help me avoid my tendency to wander off topic at times.

My Georgia Tech colleagues Bill Rouse, Rahul Basole, Sherry Farrugia and Steve Rushing all read the final draft and, hopefully, found the last few remaining wording problems and factual errors. Any they missed are, of course, entirely my responsibility.

"Medical schools should hold their graduates responsible for their medical records no matter where they may be. Indeed if they were to survey the performance of their graduates through their records they would help community hospitals with their standards and begin to get some feed-back on all the medical education programmes underway. In addition, records on a large scale would become available for computer analysis."

– Larry L. Weed, MD (1964)
Medical Records, Patient Care,
and Medical Education,
Ir J Med Sci. 462:271-82

Contents

Chapter 1
Healthcare Delivery in the US

The United States has a uniquely complex and expensive healthcare system. We are alone among the industrialized countries in not having a "single payer" or at least a single entity responsible for making the rules. As a result, each individual health provider[3] may have to deal with dozens of different health plans, each tailored by the patient's employer to try to manage rising health costs. This complexity adds significantly to administrative costs which are estimated at 25-30% of spending. One study suggests that US healthcare administrative costs at 31% are proportionately nearly twice those in Canada. [1] Many studies show that we spend around twice as much on healthcare as compared to our peer nations. Yet we get relatively poor results, particularly for routine public health issues and for managing chronic diseases, the problems that affect most people and drive most healthcare costs. It is beyond the scope of this book to examine the merits of the various proposed solutions to these problems but the belief that it can help with them is the core rationale for federal funding of the deployment of health informatics.

The Chronic Disease Problem

Most Americans think of healthcare in terms of dramatic, high-technology, life-saving interventions. It's what they see on television; it's what they hear about when a friend, neighbor, relative or celebrity develops cancer or some other serious condition. Arguably, the US has the best system for providing that sort of care, as shown in Fig. 1.1. Patients here needing what Intermountain Health's Dr. Brent James, a national thought leader in health quality improvement, calls "rescue care" have a better chance of survival than in other advanced industrialized nations.

---

[3] I have generally used the more inclusive term "provider" in preference to "physician". Provider includes physicians and other professionals such as dentists, nurses and nurse practitioners and, increasingly, care coordinators. The major exception is cases where I feel a system is quite specifically designed for use by physicians.

M.L. Braunstein, *Health Informatics in the Cloud*, SpringerBriefs in Computer Science, DOI 10.1007/978-1-4614-5629-2_1, © The Author(s) 2013

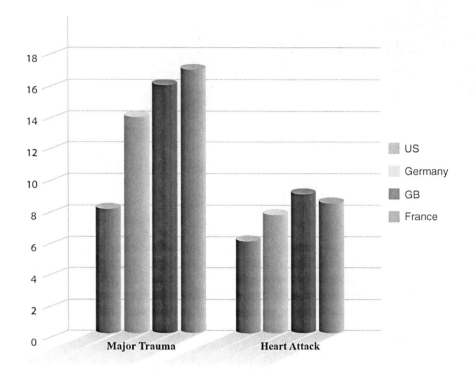

Fig. 1.1   Mortality in Life Threatening Situations (lower is better) *adapted from and courtesy of Dr. Brent James of Intermountain Health*

However, well over 90% of Medicare spending is for patients with chronic diseases such as diabetes, hypertension and coronary artery disease. [2] I'm aware of unpublished data that suggests that around 70% of spending for younger families whose care is paid for by an employer is due to chronic disease. Key economic differences between the acute high technology care we excel at here in the US and the care of chronic disease are that chronic disease care takes place mostly outside hospitals, uses little advanced medical technology and is, therefore, relatively inexpensive and less profitable for hospitals and providers.

While inexpensive to treat directly, if not managed well, chronic diseases cause complications that are expensive to treat. For example, poorly controlled hypertension can lead to stroke, heart attack or kidney failure. Moreover, chronic diseases can cause other chronic diseases. Diabetes, for example, is a major risk factor for heart disease. This compounds the cost problem because those patients with multiple conditions account for a much greater proportionate share of spending. [2]

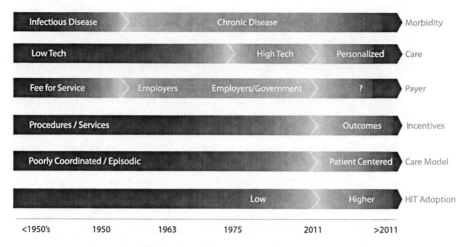

Infectious Disease		Chronic Disease			Morbidity
Low Tech		High Tech		Personalized	Care
Fee for Service	Employers	Employers/Government		?	Payer
Procedures / Services				Outcomes	Incentives
Poorly Coordinated / Episodic				Patient Centered	Care Model
		Low		Higher	HIT Adoption
<1950's	1950	1963	1975	2011	>2011

Fig. 1.2 The Evolution of US Healthcare Over the Past Few Decades

The US healthcare system is poorly designed to manage chronic disease, in large part for historic reasons (Fig. 1.2).[4] For millennia morbidity was mostly due to infectious diseases. In the 20th Century life expectancy increased substantially as a result of improved public health and sanitation, vaccinations and the antibiotics that became widely available after World War II. In the past few decades lifestyles here in the US became more sedentary and highly caloric, fast and processed food became a larger part of the American diet leading to a striking growth in obesity, a major cause of chronic disease. Today, only a few decades from when most people died of infections, the "single greatest cause of rising healthcare spending in the U.S. is the growing *prevalence* [emphasis mine] of chronic disease." [3] That point is worth re-emphasizing. Here in the US we have a *much higher rate* of chronic disease than in other countries. It is *the* health problem driving the largest share of increasing healthcare costs.

However, despite these substantial changes in disease patterns, the healthcare system remains relatively unchanged. A core reason is the nature of current economic incentives. For example, "Medicare continues to operate under a fee-for-service model, which complicates the adoption of chronic care treatment models." [2] In most communities healthcare is dominated by the local hospital, a place where little of the care for chronic disease can or should be done. Physicians offering high technology procedures and treatments make far more money than those offering primary care, the mainstay of chronic disease management.

---

[4] For these, among other reasons, we compare poorly to the other industrialized countries in many measures of health and public health in particular. For the official statistics on this visit http://stats.oecd.org/ and click on Health Status.

Any medical student already knows this. Primary care physicians such as family doctors, general internists, pediatricians and gynecologists can expect to make far less than they would earn as a surgeon or specialist. [4] As a result, we have a shortage of primary care physicians, the front line warriors in the battle against chronic disease. [5] To leverage those scarce resources and achieve better results requires a different approach than the traditional physician-centric, episodic office visit with little or no contact with the patient managing their disease at home between these visits.

Why a different approach? Consider any acute, life-threatening problem. It is likely to be diagnosed and treated within a relatively short period of time. The care will often take place in *one* highly specialized venue where care coordination, though hardly guaranteed, is substantially simpler and the patient is essentially a passive participant.

Contrast that to a diagnosis of chronic disease which, by definition, is not curable. Treatment will take place over years or even decades in multiple venues that may be widely geographically dispersed. The complexity of coordinating care is compounded with multiple chronic diseases, particularly in our highly fragmented and specialized system of care. So "while the average Medicare beneficiary sees between six and seven different physicians, **beneficiaries with five or more chronic conditions see almost 14 different physicians in a year** [emphasis mine] and average 37 physician visits annually". People with five or more chronic conditions fill almost 50 prescriptions in a year. [6] In fact "virtually all of the [Medicare] spending growth since 1987 can be traced to patients treated for five or more conditions." [2]

Success in treating chronic disease depends heavily on the behavior of patients *when they are outside of what is traditionally thought of as the healthcare system.* Not only are these diseases often caused by issues such as poor diet and lack of exercise but proper diet, exercise and medication compliance is almost always critical to successfully managing them. New technologies such as the Internet and wireless and mobile devices are of great interest because of their potential to engage these patients at home and change their behavior both to prevent and more successfully manage chronic disease.

Health Data Logistics

"Our healthcare system needs all the help it can get. And health information technology is some of the best medicine we have."

– Tommy G. Thompson [7]

Among the key problems for which information technology is clearly good medicine is insufficient data sharing among the many care providers treating patients with chronic diseases, particularly those with multiple diseases. According to the IOM, the "fact that more than 40 percent of people with chronic conditions have more than one such condition argues strongly for more sophisticated mechanisms to communicate and coordinate care. Yet physician groups, hospitals, and other healthcare organizations operate as silos, often providing care without the benefit of complete information about the patient's condition, medical history, services provided in other settings, or medications prescribed by other clinicians." [8]

The practice of medicine is largely comprised of collecting data, analyzing that data, making decisions based on it, conveying those decisions to other members of a care team and the patient, following what happens, and adjusting according. Any effective coordination of care depends on making a patient's data available when and where it is needed. In essence, we have a "health data logistics problem". That is what the national effort to deploy health informatics is primarily aimed at solving.

This is very analogous to problems other industries have identified and solved using contemporary information technology. For example, Wal-Mart famously scans every item sold in its stores and transmits the information, as sales occur, to databases at its Arkansas headquarters where it is virtually instantaneously available for analysis and action. If snow shovels are fast sellers in Minnesota, Wal-Mart makes sure more are on the way. If swim suits are languishing in Florida, it slows their resupply. Wal-Mart can only do this because it has a standard electronic record of every sales transaction and a network in place to seamlessly and quickly move that digital information from where it is generated to where it is needed.

Countless manufacturers have similar systems in place to manage a global supply chain and logistics network feeding components to their plants. This is the sort of technology that makes "just in time" possible. Today most automobile manufacturers rely on suppliers to deliver entire and often even customized subassemblies as they are needed for installation in a particular car. Their computer systems are integrated with those of the companies that supply them so the entire process can be orchestrated efficiently without error or delay.

Paper records are hard to share. The original can physically exist in only one place. They can be copied and faxed but this is slow, time consuming and relatively error prone. The results may not be very legible. The information contained in them is rarely standardized except where required for billing.

Yet, in many respects, managing chronic disease is a "data logistics problem" comparable to those we just described. More effective management of these increasingly common problems will depend to a large degree on creating the same data liquidity that drives all current global logistics and supply chains. Of great, or perhaps even equal, importance is the need to substantially improve care processes based on this wider access to more timely and accurate data.

Consider a seemingly simple issue: when should a chronic disease patient next be seen by their physician? The traditional approach is somewhat arbitrary but is hopefully guided by experience and intuition. The next appointment is scheduled in three months, six months or a year. If Wal-Mart used this approach of stocking their inventory on a fixed schedule unneeded swim suits might arrive at Florida stores even though the shelves are overflowing. Potential sales of snow shovels in Minnesota might be lost as customers go elsewhere because the inventory is exhausted.

Perhaps Mr. Smith, a diabetic patient who just saw his physician, will do fine. He will follow the prescribed diet and take his medications in the proper amount and at the proper time. If so, he won't need to be seen in six months, as scheduled, but, in most clinics, the physician will see him anyway, congratulate him on his success and schedule the next visit after another six months.

At the same time Mrs. Jones, the hypertensive patient who came in right after Mr. Smith, decides she is feeling fine and does not need her medications which, after all, are quite expensive on her limited budget. Two months before her scheduled return visit she suffers a stroke and ends up in the hospital and, after discharge, requires months of expensive, painful care and rehabilitation.

Healthcare deals poorly with these patients in large part because traditional practice models only deal with them during visits. This provider-centric, office-based view of care is partly historic and largely the result of our reimbursement system. Physicians have normally only been paid when they *physically* see patients. Moreover, unlike Wal-Mart and the auto manufacturers, care providers typically don't have a "real time" view of how their patients are doing.

A "data logistics" approach would capture data at the source – the home – and transmit it to where it is needed so Mr. Smith is not brought back for an un-needed visit and Mrs. Jones is brought back when her hypertension is clearly starting to get out of control, possibly preventing her stroke.

Changing Processes

"The hospital is altogether the most complex human organization ever devised."
                                                                    – Peter Drucker [9]

The IOM goes on to say that "If we want safer, higher-quality care, we will need to have redesigned systems of care" which "must be designed to serve the needs of patients, and to ensure that they are fully informed, retain control and participate in care delivery whenever possible, and receive care that is respectful of their values and preferences." Finally, it recognized the critical importance of improved management of chronic disease which it said "needs to be a collaborative, multidisciplinary process." [8]

The IOM identified six challenges healthcare organizations would face in developing these new care systems. The first was "to redesign care processes to serve more effectively the needs of the chronically ill for coordinated, seamless care across settings and clinicians and over time." [8]

We've seen that information technology has been utilized by many other industries to transform business processes. Consider another example from an organization that is not typically associated with high technology – the US Postal Service (USPS®). We all dread going to the post office to send packages, particularly during busy holiday periods. The predictable waiting line is a major factor that drives many individual consumers to use a UPS® or FEDEX® store, even if they are more expensive. So, in response, the USPS has introduced "Click-N-Ship®". Go to their website, answer a few questions and print the bar coded shipping label. Once it is attached to the package you can go to the head of the line and drop your package off at the counter and leave without any interaction with the clerk.

This is a transformed business process only possible through an innovative application of technology. Make things convenient and people are more likely to use them. Hopefully, you can see that it has many similarities to the data logistics approach to chronic disease described at the end of the previous section. Among these are the use of the Internet to bridge time and space by taking advantage of the availability of technology in the home. Most importantly, both depend on the willingness to "think outside the box" with respect to how we do business. If the USPS can do it, why can't the healthcare system?

Perverse Incentives

"A problem is something you have hopes of changing. Anything else is a fact of life."
– C R Smith [10]

The answer has a lot to do with financial incentives. If the USPS can transfer the entire package preparation and drop off function to the consumer, they reap any resulting financial benefits. It costs less to process the package because their customer is doing much of the work. Their customer is more likely to use their service because it is more convenient.

Though there are clear financial benefits to avoiding unnecessary care, the beneficiary is usually the employer that insures their own health benefit, an insurance company or government. In most circumstances, if a physician uses technology to avoid unnecessary care, visits to the emergency department or hospitalizations, the physician's income is certainly not increased and may even be diminished. Moreover, any time spent by staff using some new technology-mediated process may represent lost income. To make matters even worse, up until very recently, if a practice wanted to utilize technology to facilitate an innovative care model, it would bear the entire investment.

This conundrum, in which there is a mismatch between who has to invest and who might benefit, is characteristic of what my colleague, Bill Rouse, and others refer to as a "complex adaptive system". [11] In such a system there are multiple "independent agents" each of whom are intelligent, adapt to changing conditions and act to optimize their own self-interest. Moreover, no entity is in control.

So, despite the availability of enabling technology to transform healthcare, adoption would continue to lag without incentives to bridge the self-interests of the independent agents. Solutions have been tried for decades. For example, in a health maintenance organization (HMO) employers typically contract for the care of their employees on a fixed annual basis. If the care costs more, the HMO has to make up the difference and loses money. If it costs less, the HMO benefits financially. This is a clear example of trying to change incentives. This contrasts sharply with traditional fee-for-service model where providers typically make more money the more services they provide. There is room to argue about whether the fee-for-service approach leads to the delivery of unneeded services but few could argue that it provides a disincentive to invest in technologies to replace traditional approaches to services that can be reimbursed with new technology-based alternatives that are not.

A landmark 2008 survey of 2,758 physicians [12] strongly supports this conclusion. Despite the long time availability of electronic health record systems with the capability to improve clinical decision making and expedite the management of prescriptions and other orders, in 2008 only 4% of physicians had a "fully functional" system that could do those things. At the top of the reasons given for not having one were the cost and the uncertainty about achieving a return on the investment. Interestingly, physicians who had implemented such a system had a high degree of satisfaction and saw clinical benefits to their patients, a part of the survey not as often cited as the low adoption numbers. Some might be tempted to be critical of physicians based on this, but they are acting rationally and exactly as the theory of a complex adaptive system predicts – in a manner to maximize their own perceived self-interest.

Fixing this requires new incentives. In our highly fragmented health system usually only Medicare which, according to MEDPAC (the advisor to Congress on Medicare issues), paid for some 23% of personal healthcare spending in 2010 [13], has the size and market presence to introduce transformative change. This study and other data led to the decision by the federal government to essentially pay the cost of electronic health record technology in provider offices and hospitals *if* those systems are used in a manner called "Meaningful Use" that could transform care, at least modestly. In parallel, the Affordable Care Act of 2010 introduced Medicare Accountable Care Organizations (ACO), to create financial incentives, similar to those in an HMO, but utilizing a contractual arrangement with existing community-based care providers. Many major private health insurance companies are now also adapting a similar model. The needed new incentives may now be in place. We turn to them next.

References

1. Woolhandler S, Campbell T and Himmelstein DU (2003) Costs of Healthcare Administration in the United States and Canada. N Engl J Med; 349:768–775
2. Thorpe KE and Howard DH (2006) The Rise In Spending Among Medicare Beneficiaries: The Role Of Chronic Disease Prevalence and Changes in Treatment Intensity. Health Affairs 25 (2006): w378–w388
3. Kumar S and Nigmatullin A (2010) Exploring the impact of management of chronic illnesses through prevention on the U.S. healthcare delivery system – A closed loop system's modeling study. Information Knowledge Systems Management 9:127–152
4. Medscape Physician Compensation Report: 2011 http://www.medscape.com/features/slideshow/compensation/2011/ Accessed 19 July 2012
5. http://www.kaiseredu.org/Issue-Modules/Primary-Care-Shortage/Background-Brief.aspx Accessed 19 July 2012
6. Anderson G and Horvath J (2004) The Growing Burden of Chronic Disease in America. Public Health Reports 119:May–June 2004
7. http://www.hhs.gov/news/speech/2004/040721.html Accessed 19 July 2012
8. Committee on Quality of Healthcare in America (2001) Crossing the Quality Chasm: A New Health System for the 21st Century. The National Academies Press
9. Drucker P (2002) They're Not Employees, They're People. Harvard Business Review
10. Smith CR (1969) Publishers Weekly, September 8, 1969
11. Rouse WB (2008) Healthcare as a Complex Adaptive System. The Bridge, Vol. 38, Issue 1, pp. 17–25
12. DesRoches CM *et al* (2008) Electronic Health Records in Ambulatory Care— A National Survey of Physicians. N Engl J Med 359:50-60
13. http://www.medpac.gov/documents/Jun12DataBookEntireReport.pdf Accessed 15 September 2012

Chapter 2
Federal Policies and Initiatives

A number of new federal initiatives are designed to promote the adoption of electronic health records and health information exchange, and to create new care models and processes for chronic disease management enabled by these technologies. The health informatics efforts are being managed by the Office of the National Coordinator for Health Information Technology (ONC), a new federal agency created by the Bush administration to implement the goal of universal adoption of electronic health records by 2014. Major commercial health insurers have adopted their own versions of some of these programs, suggesting their impact will be health system wide. Even though I describe these initiatives separately, it is important to consider their potential cumulative effect.

Certified Electronic Health Records

First, we need to deal with a terminology issue. Early on the term "electronic medical record" (EMR) was used to designate a computer-based patient chart. At that time the focus was generally only on the physician. Technologies like the Internet offer the prospect of engaging all stakeholders, including the patient, in a networked healthcare system where data is shared and a more complete clinical and behavioral picture is available to all. This complete picture is now called the "electronic health record" (EHR). The EMR is a component of it. It also represents a shift in mindset away from treating disease and toward maintaining health. [1]

The federal "Meaningful Use" program we will discuss next requires that providers ("eligible professionals") install a certified EHR. A detailed discussion of certification is beyond the scope of this book, but a section of the final rule published by ONC provides a working definition: "An electronic record of health-related information on an individual that: (A) Includes patient demographic and clinical health information, such as medical history and problem lists; and (B) has the capacity: (i) to provide clinical decision support; (ii) to support physician order entry; (iii) to capture and query information relevant to healthcare quality; and

M.L. Braunstein, *Health Informatics in the Cloud*, SpringerBriefs in Computer Science, DOI 10.1007/978-1-4614-5629-2_2, © The Author(s) 2013

(iv) to exchange electronic health information with, and integrate such information from other sources." [2]

ONC has approved six organizations to do certification testing and 1,426 certified products are listed on their website. Of these, 924 are "complete EHRs" meaning a purchase of this system alone provides all the tools to achieve Meaningful Use. The rest are "modular EHRs" meaning that they can be combined with other modular components to achieve Meaningful Use. An example of a modular EHR would be a system for e-prescribing. It would need to be combined with at least one other module that could provide the rest of the required functionality. This complexity and multiplicity of choices creates a problem for prospective purchasers. ONC provides an online "shopping tool" [3] but no real substantive guidance. For providers seeking such advice I offer some suggestions in Resources at the end of the book.

Meaningful Use

In 2008 DesRoches *et al* published a comprehensive physician EHR adoption survey and introduced the distinction between "basic" electronic health record systems and "fully functional" systems. [4] Table 1 of the paper [5] describes in detail the difference between a "passive" electronic replacement for paper charts and a system that "actively" intervenes to help improve care quality. It provides a useful basis for understanding the concept of Meaningful Use as defined by ONC.

The American Recovery and Reconstruction Act (ARRA, the "Stimulus") that is funding EHR deployment defines Meaningful Use as including three components:

1. The use of a certified EHR in a meaningful manner.
2. The electronic exchange of health information to improve quality of healthcare.
3. The use of certified EHR technology to submit clinical quality and other measures.

ONC was charged to define what a certified EHR is and to develop a process for certifying EHRs. It was also told by Congress to more specifically define and implement Meaningful Use of those certified EHRs. After much debate and the solicitation of external input, ONC decided to do this in three stages (Fig. 2.1).

The ARRA program funds adoption by hospitals and community-based "eligible providers". Eligible providers are physicians and a list of other licensed health professionals. Hospitals and eligible providers each have their own Meaningful Use standards but we'll only discuss the standards for eligible providers.

At present Stages 1 and 2 have been finalized. As shown in Fig. 2.1, Stage 1 focuses on data collection and sharing while Stage 2 introduces more advanced uses of that data to improve clinical processes and decisions. Both stages require the

---

[5] http://www.nejm.org/doi/full/10.1056/NEJMsa0802005

Stage 1	Stage 2	Stage 3
2011-2012	**2013**	**2015**
Data capture and sharing	Advance clinical processes	Improved outcomes

Stage 1: Meaningful use criteria focus on:	Stage 2: Meaningful use criteria focus on:	Stage 3: Meaningful use criteria focus on:
Electronically capturing health information in a standardized format	More rigorous health information exchange (HIE)	Improving quality, safety, and efficiency, leading to improved health outcomes
Using that information to track key clinical conditions	Increased requirements for e-prescribing and incorporating lab results	Decision support for national high-priority conditions
Communicating that information for care coordination processes	Electronic transmission of patient care summaries across multiple settings	Patient access to self-management tools
Initiating the reporting of clinical quality measures and public health information	More patient-controlled data	Access to comprehensive patient data through patient-centered HIE
Using information to engage patients and their families in their care		Improving population health

Fig. 2.1 The Three Stages of Meaningful Use

submission of certain quality measures. Defining quality and appropriate measures is itself a complex subject. For our purposes it suffices to recognize that quality measures are typically either of *process* (did the provider frequently enough do something that is desired) or of *outcome* (did enough of the provider's patients achieve a desired result).

The quality measures in Stage 1 are divided into 15 mandatory **Core Measures** a so-called **Menu Set** of 10 measures of which 5 must be done, 3 core **Clinical Quality Measures** and 38 optional quality measures of which 3 must be done. The Core and Menu Set measures are further subdivided into groups of measures. The groups and examples provided here use language taken directly from the government and may contain unfamiliar terms.

The Stage 1 **Core Measures** are divided into four groups and are mostly measures of process. The four groups are listed below along with an example of one of the quality measures for each group.

Improve Quality, Safety, and Efficiency, and Reduce Health Disparities

Example: At least 40% of prescriptions transmitted electronically to the patient's pharmacy.

Engage Patients and Families

Example: Provide patients clinical summaries within three business days for more than 50 percent of all office visits.

Improve Care Coordination

Example: Perform at least one test to demonstrate the ability to exchange key clinical information with other providers.

Privacy and Security

Example: Conduct or review a security risk analysis and implement security updates as necessary.

The ten Stage 1 Menu Set measures are also divided into four groups. These measures are not all mandatory; each provider must implement at least five. Again, here is one example for each of the four groups:

Improve Quality, Safety, and Efficiency, and Reduce Health Disparities

Example: Generate at least one report listing patients with a specific condition.

Engage Patients and Families

Example: Send reminders, if desired, for preventive/follow-up care for specified minimum percentages of adult and pediatric patients

Improve Care Coordination

Example: Perform medication reconciliation for more than 50 percent of patient transitions into the care of the physician.

Improve Population and Public Health

Example: Perform at least one test of EHR's capability to provide electronic syndromic surveillance data to public health agencies, and perform a follow-up submission if the test is successful.

The three core Clinical Quality measures relate to: 1) adult weight screening; 2) screening and management of hypertension and; 3) determining smoking behavior and prescribing cessation measures if appropriate. The Stage 1 and Stage 2 requirements and the full set of quality measures are summarized clearly on the Internet. [5]

In general Stage 2 raises the bar on performance requiring, for example, more health information exchange, increased e-prescribing and electronic access to digital scans and images. Of particular interest are two new Core Measures requiring that 5% of a provider's patients actually access their health data electronically and that an equal percentage send secure electronic messages to their provider. As we'll see later on, these new core measures promote wider use of Personal Health Records and the new DIRECT approach to health information exchange. At least one useful comparison of the three stages in chart form is posted on the Internet. [6]

The specifics are the subject of debate, discussion, and negotiation. However, even a casual inspection of these examples should reveal how closely they align with the data logistic problems of chronic disease management. They are clearly designed to move electronic health record system vendors and their customers from "basic" to "fully functional" use of the technology. Finally, in many cases, they align well with the original arguments made by Dr. Larry Weed for electronic records back in the 1960's and quoted in part at the beginning of the book.

The Medicare and Medicaid EHR Incentive Programs

These are complex programs we won't cover broadly here. There is an official site [7] and a good article that summarizes the programs for health providers. [8] Providers are termed "eligible professionals". The definition of this is different under the Medicare and Medicaid incentive programs but extends beyond licensed physicians in both. Eligible professionals can be reimbursed for their investment in a certified electronic health record system up to $44,000 over five years under the Medicare EHR Incentive Program and up to $63,750 over six years under the Medicaid program.

There are criteria for whether or not a provider practice is eligible based on their volume of Medicare or Medicaid patients. Providers cannot participate in both programs. Medicare is run by the federal government so it is uniform across the country. Medicaid is run by each state with some funding from the federal government so, as with all Medicaid policies, the details can vary by state. Those providers who do not achieve Meaningful Use by 2015 will see a downward adjustment in their Medicare payments. The amount of this adjustment will grow through 2020 when it will reach 5%. There are currently no payment adjustments under the Medicaid program.

These incentive programs were clearly designed to resolve the incentive disconnect with respect to who invests in electronic records and who benefits from them. In other words, the federal government acknowledges that the main beneficiaries will be the organizations that pay for healthcare – primarily the government itself and employers providing health insurance. As a result, the government will cover the investment for eligible professionals who install electronic records and use them in a manner that should, at least in theory, improve the quality and efficiency of healthcare. The final tally is still years off, but adoption has clearly increased and I believe this substantial investment is also paying off in ways that weren't necessarily predicted up front. It has become a driver for innovation. We will look at specific examples of these innovative new technologies in Chapters 4 through 7.

Accountable Care Organizations

The idea of producing better results while spending less may seem counterintuitive to some readers. However, it is a key assumption in most quality improvement efforts and is well accepted in other industries, such as manufacturing, where doing it right the first time, rather than inspecting for defects and fixing them after the fact, has led to substantive improvements in product quality while driving down costs.

Healthcare, as always, is different. An example of this is found in a 2004 study from Kaiser Permanente. [9] It looked at disease management programs for coronary artery disease, heart failure, diabetes, and asthma in their organization and found that "we cannot reduce costs by improving quality unless the treatments and educational interventions that we bring to the chronically ill are not merely recommended by evidence-based guidelines but are cost-saving."

To achieve cost savings we need new care models designed to reduce cost. Such models do exist. The Robert Wood Johnson foundation advocates the Chronic Care Model [10]. The American Academy of Pediatrics, the American Academy of Family Physicians (and its Transformed subsidiary) and other groups advocate the Patient Centered Medical Home (PCMH). [11] These are similar models that emphasize a more coordinated and team-oriented approach to care that ultimately requires health information technology to manage and orchestrate new processes.

They do seem to work, if done properly. A review article found that "18 of 27 studies of the Chronic Care model concerned with 3 examples of chronic conditions (congestive heart failure, asthma, and diabetes) demonstrated reduced healthcare costs or lower use of healthcare services." [12]

The term "Accountable Care Organization" (ACO) was first used in 2006 by Elliott Fisher, Director of the Center for Health Policy Research at Dartmouth Medical School, during a discussion at a public meeting of the Medicare Payment Advisory Commission. [13] Again, we will not delve into the details here but an article from Health Affairs [14] provides a good overview. The basic idea is to change the reimbursement model so that practitioners are rewarded for providing care at or above well-defined levels of quality *if* they do this at a lower cost than would otherwise be expected. Will this approach work?

ACOs are designed to help solve some of the basic deficiencies in our management of chronic disease by incentivizing providers to adopt the new models for chronic disease management. As we discussed earlier, one of the major problems is lack of information sharing. Chronic disease drives the substantial majority of healthcare costs. Given the fragmented nature of our health system chronic disease patients – particularly those with multiple chronic diseases – receive care from many different providers in the typical year. In this country, except in certain limited areas that do have a health information exchange, each provider delivers care with little or no knowledge of what the other providers have done.

But does this lack of data sharing actually create problems? The answer seems to be yes. The 2008 Commonwealth Fund International Health Policy Survey of Sicker Adults [15] was a telephone survey conducted from March to May 2008 of prescreened adults whose health was fair or poor based on; serious illness in past

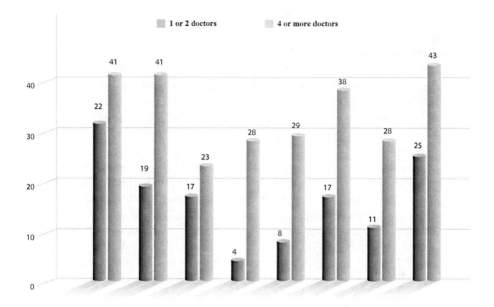

Fig. 2.2 More Physicians Caring for a Patient Can Lead to More Errors

2 years; or who were hospitalized; or had major surgery in past 2 years. The study showed that, among other results, specialists see patients without having their medical records around 20% of the time and that 30% of patients are discharged from hospitals without specific medication instructions. In sum, as shown in Fig. 2.2, 43% of these patients reported a medical mistake, medication error, and/or lab test error or delay when they were seen by four or more physicians versus 25% by those who were seen by 1 or 2 physicians.

The details are again beyond the scope of this book and, in part, are not yet clear, but an ACO offers to share savings with a self-organized provider group so long as it also produces quality measures at or above some pre-defined level. In practice the group might be a hospital and physician practices it owns or collaborates with. It might be medical practices, home health and long term care providers and pharmacists who band together using health information technology to deliver more coordinated care.

Much of the belief that this approach can work comes from a pilot program in ten large physician group practices (PGPs) begun in 2005 and funded by the Centers for Medicare & Medicaid Services (CMS), the huge federal agency that manages both the Medicare program to provide healthcare for the elderly and the Medicaid program for the poor and people with certain disabilities. The purpose was "to examine whether care management initiatives could generate cost savings by reducing avoidable hospital admissions, readmissions, and emergency department visits, while improving quality results". [16] All PGPs met at least 29 of the 32 quality goals, most of which were process measures related to coronary artery disease, diabetes, heart failure, hypertension, and preventive care. Five generated Medicare savings of $38.7 million, earning performance payments of $31.7 million. Marshfield Clinic, a well known and respected health system in Wisconsin, was the most successful site and earned more than half of the performance payments. Dr. Theodore Praxel, who headed the Marshfield effort, attributed their success in part to "health information technology (point-of-care reminders, being completely chartless)".

A report on this project by the Commonwealth Fund states that:

"All of the sites participating in the PGP Demonstration have introduced some form of information technology that makes clinical data more readily available at the point of care, including EHRs and patient registries. This supports the introduction of planned visits.

These systems have improved workflow efficiencies in several ways without requiring new hires or taxing current staff. EHRs can include abnormality prompts that indicate to a provider that certain tests are missing for a particular patient. These types of prompts can improve the workflow as well as quality of care. One site includes each of the three components of the diabetic foot exam in its EHR." [17]

So, success under an ACO does appear to increase if health information technology is used appropriately. From a provider perspective, however, this requires a substantial investment beyond whatever money is paid by the incentive programs *if* they are successful in meeting the requirements for extra reimbursement. In addition to the technology, new care models need to be put in place and this can require additional space or renovations of existing space, retraining of employees as well as hiring new kinds of employees such as care coordinators.

Reflecting on this would suggest that a health system that makes this investment would be better off if the cost could be spread out among as many patients as possible so that the benefits of success would be greater. The opportunity to do this seems to be growing as most of the major private insurers are following the trend that Medicare has started with outcome-based payment systems of their own. [18] [19] [20] [21]

Two of them have gone far beyond that. In 2010 UnitedHealth acquired Axolotl (now called OptunInsight), the largest supplier of HIE technology, and Aetna acquired Medicity, the second largest supplier. These two companies obviously see health informatics as such a strategic tool for managing outcome-based care that they want to provide the tools themselves, presumably to create competitive advantage.

Taken together these new Federal programs create incentives for providers to deploy electronic medical records and utilize them, along with health information exchange, to manage new care models that improve quality while reducing costs. At least that is the hope. The results are far from clear but I'm optimistic they will be positive, if the programs are fairly designed in a manner that allows providers to experiment and find models that work for them locally and if they are given a sufficient chance to work in our highly charged and polarized health political environment.[6]

---

[6] For an excellent discussion of the ACO concept from all the major perspectives, I strongly recommend you read the report by the Taconic Health Information Network and Community (THINC) in the Hudson Valley of NY State. [22]

References

1. Garets D and Davis M (2006) Electronic Medical Records vs. Electronic Health Records: Yes, There Is a Difference. HIMMS Analytics http://www.himssanalytics.org/docs/WP_EMR_EHR.pdf Accessed 19 July, 2012
2. Dimick, C Meaningful Use and EHR Certification (2010) http://journal.ahima.org/2010/09/02/meaningful-use-and-ehr-certification/ Accessed 19 July, 2012
3. http://oncchpl.force.com/ehrcert?q=CHPL Accessed 19 July, 2012
4. DesRoches CM, et al (2008) Electronic Health Records in Ambulatory Care— A National Survey of Physicians. N Engl J Med 359:50–60
5. http://www.healthit.gov/providers-professionals/how-attain-meaningful-use Accessed 23 September, 2012
6. http://www.advisory.com/Research/IT-Strategy-Council/Resources/Posters/2012/Meaningful-use-the-whiteboard-story Accessed 23 September, 2012
7. http://ehrincentives.cms.gov/hitech/login.action
8. Kibbe DC (2010) A Physician's Guide to the Medicare and Medicaid EHR Incentive Programs: The Basics. Fam Pract Manag. 17(5):17–21
9. Firemen B, Bartlett J and Selby J (2004) Can Disease Management Reduce Healthcare Costs By Improving Quality? Health Affairs, 23(6): 63–75
10. http://www.improvingchroniccare.org/ Accessed 19 July, 2012
11. http://www.transformed.com/ Accessed 19 July, 2012
12. Bodenheimer T et al, (2002) Improving Primary Care for Patients With Chronic Illness: The Chronic Care Model, Part 2. JAMA 288(15):1909–1914
13. http://content.healthaffairs.org/content/26/1/w44.full.html
14. ACOs (2011) http://www.healthaffairs.org/healthpolicybriefs/brief.php?brief_id=61 Accessed 23 September, 2012
15. Commonwealth Fund International Health Policy Survey of Sicker Adults (2008) http://www.commonwealthfund.org/Surveys/2008/2008-Commonwealth-Fund-International-Health-Policy-Survey-of-Sicker-Adults.aspx Accessed 19 July, 2012
16. Iglehart JK (2011) Assessing an ACO Prototype — Medicare's Physician Group Practice Demonstration. N Engl J Med; 364:198–200
17. Trisolini M et al (2008) The Medicare Physician Group Practice Demonstration: Lessons Learned on Improving Quality and Efficiency in Healthcare http://www.commonwealthfund.org/~1/media/Files/Publications/Fund%20;Report/2008/Feb/The%20;Medicare%20;Physician%20;Group%20;Practice%20;Demonstration%20;%20;Lessons%20;Learned%20;on%20;Improving%20;Quality%20;and%20;Effici/1094_Trisolini_Medicare_phys_group_practice_demo_lessons_learned%20;pdf.pdf Accessed 19 July, 2012
18. Newcomer LN (2012) Changing Physician Incentives For Cancer Care To Reward Better Patient Outcomes Instead Of Use Of More Costly Drugs. Health Aff 31(4):780–785
19. http://www.anthem.com/ca/health-insurance/about-us/pressreleasedetails/CA/2011/694 Accessed 23 September, 2012
20. Chase D (2012) Aetna's Remarkable Reinvention Underway http://www.forbes.com/sites/davechase/2012/03/17/aetnas-remarkable-reinvention-underway Accessed 19 July, 2012
21. Stevens S (2010) How Health Plans Can Accelerate Healthcare Innovation http://blogs.hbr.org/cs/2010/05/how_health_plans_can_accelerate.html Accessed 19 July, 2012
22. THINC (2011) Building ACOs and Outcome Based Contracting in the Commercial Market: Provider and Payor Perspectives http://www.ebglaw.com/files/47636_Hastings-Lutes-Friedberg-THINC-ACO-Report.pdf Accessed 19 July, 2012

Chapter 3
Contemporary Informatics Tools

There are many new tools, systems and approaches that comprise a contemporary approach to health informatics. Given space limitations and the enormous change in this regard in the past few years I am emphasizing those new approaches that I believe will lead us forward with little emphasis on the more traditional technologies and approaches. This is the most technical chapter in the book but it is written as simply and clearly as possible to be comprehensible to the non-technical reader.

A Quick Overview of Computing

Computers first became commercially available around 1950. Early on, it was assumed that they would be used to solve complex mathematical problems. In time, and as the technology for storing data advanced, they became increasingly important in information management. Today, while sophisticated computers forecast the weather, simulate nuclear explosions and even the molecular processes within cells, by far the most common use of computing is to collect, manipulate, store and transmit information.

Most health information management systems involve sharing data from many diverse sources within or among organizations. These systems are typically designed using a paradigm called "client-server computing" which is the architecture found today in most hospitals and larger clinics. Certain computers, called "clients", collect and display information. The client computer is the computer that providers interact with, viewing medical history or typing in new information about a patient. Other computers, called "servers", handle the information storage function for the clients. Whenever a client needs to display old information or store new information, these requests are handled by the servers. There is often a substantial physical separation of the servers, typically residing in a closet somewhere, and the clients, which are distributed throughout a hospital or clinic, so a "network" is required to connect them to each other. For the past few decades this client server paradigm has been the predominant form of computing.

M.L. Braunstein, *Health Informatics in the Cloud*, SpringerBriefs in Computer Science, DOI 10.1007/978-1-4614-5629-2_3, © The Author(s) 2013

However, important changes are taking place and may have significant positive ramifications for applying information technology to healthcare. First, client computers are increasingly mobile. Physical network connections within buildings, and, to a lesser degree, outside of them, are giving way to wireless technologies. Today, half of all computing devices are mobile. This includes "Smartphones" that are not really phones but small mobile computers with a phone packaged within them. Mobile technology is, of course, particularly attractive to workers on their feet and moving about, a category that includes many healthcare providers. I observed this back in the early 1970s where the care providers in our clinic were restrained in their use of our early EMR because they had to go to a place where a terminal was located and sit at it to enter or retrieve information. The paper chart, on the other hand, was something they could hold and carry around with them.

A second major change is the Internet. We use it so frequently that we take it for granted and do not often stop to think about what it is. The idea that a computer network could be a general purpose vehicle for data communications dates to the early 1960's. [1] By the late 1960's such a network connected four research labs. Eventually this led to the Internet, a commercial open network first operated in the mid-1990s. It is hard to think of any technology that has been more rapidly and widely adopted. Today, not quite twenty years later, Internet connected devices are a routine part of daily living for billions of people around the planet. Though the Internet is also based on "client-server architecture", the clients and servers are distributed throughout the world. The client in the Internet is a personal computer (or increasingly a Smartphone) running a web browser such as Internet Explorer, Safari, Chrome or Firefox. The information that is transmitted, stored and retrieved is much more general purpose and can derive from any one of millions of servers – anything from bank information to a blog post to a weather forecast. A web server or servers is responsible for managing the information storage and retrieval for each web page that makes up the Internet, and the browser connects to multiple servers as a person navigates from page to page.

Taken together, along with the miniaturization of servers that can now be stacked together in massive quantities in a central facility, these innovations facilitate a computing paradigm that appears to be replacing the traditional client-server architecture. It is referred to as "cloud computing" and the ultimate goal is to make computing resources much less expensive and as easy to access as other utilities such as water and electricity. Companies like Amazon, Google and Microsoft have constructed extremely large data centers and offer cloud computing on a usage basis. Their customers need only purchase client devices to utilize any of the services available from the numerous vendors whose offerings are hosted in their cloud service. We need some more details to understand how cloud computing differs from client-server computing since both use the same core elements of clients, servers and a network.

Traditional client-server systems are implemented in technology designed for that purpose. They generally assume a very fast network connection between the clients and the server and they assume they are in direct control of the screen for display and collection of information. The software in these systems is often very proprietary (there are clear and even major exceptions including the Linux operating system, the

My SQL database technology and the Veteran's Administration's VistA enterprise information system). Their technology comes from an era where data sharing among independently developed systems was not much of a consideration and, as a result, they tend to have significant interoperability problems.

While there is nothing inherently wrong with client-server, true cloud-based systems are developed in technologies designed to operate on the web. They can deal with the much slower connection speed between clients and the servers. They are designed to operate within a web browser. They may well be designed using standard components and tools which facilitate the sort of interconnections among web pages you're used to on the Internet. For example, it is not unusual for the content on a single web page to actually derive from different servers that may be operated by different organizations. They are also much more often "open source" meaning that further development of the technology is done be a community rather than one vendor. The hope, of course, is that this approach will be less expensive and more closely align the technology with the needs of the entire community of users.

To give an example, data from a blood pressure device in a patient's home and that actually resides on a server operated by the company that builds the device might be viewed within a patient chart developed by a cloud-based EHR company. To the provider viewing the chart that would be transparent, it would all look like one system. In fact, data from the device at home might even be graphed along with blood pressure readings taken by the provider during office visits to give a more complete view of the patient's status over time.

There can also be major advantages to using the web when all utilization of a service goes to one system that can then learn and improve from its collective experience. This sort of arrangement is virtually non-existent in traditional client-server computing but is commonplace on the web and is much more directly supported by technologies for web development.

Cloud computing may be a particularly attractive idea for smaller physician practices where the challenges of operating physical servers and networks can be formidable and economically unattractive. However, cloud computing is increasingly also being used by large enterprises. Companies in the UK [2] and India [3] have announced cloud-based hospital information systems. Of more direct relevance to this book and some of its readers, several cloud-based EHRs are commercially available.

Health Information Exchange (HIE)

Earlier we discussed the data logistics problems faced by healthcare, particularly in the management of chronic disease. We also explained the evidence that sharing of clinical data among providers may be a key strategy toward improving the quality and efficiency of care.

Health data is highly confidential and is protected by the Health Insurance Portability and Accountability Act of 1996 (HIPAA) which mandates severe penalties, including prison time, for violations. The law specifically addresses Protected Health Information (PHI) which is any health information, demographic or claims data that can be specifically linked to a patient. Sharing of PHI among providers requires special safeguards and technologies specifically crafted to support these requirements. Recently technology to support sharing of clinical information has undergone significant transitions to approaches that take advantage of the Internet and cloud computing.

Broadly speaking the technology models for Health Information Exchange (HIE) are either "centralized" or "federated". The centralized model is similar in many respects to client-server computing. It is implemented in something similar to a hub and spoke arrangement in which each EHR in the geographic area being served sends and receives the information to be shared through a central system. In contrast, under a federated model there is a minimal central system.

A centralized HIE has many advantages, particularly if it can translate among EHRs that use different terminologies to represent similar clinical concepts. The premier example of this approach in the US is the Indiana Health Information Exchange (IHIE) that connects over 90 hospitals, long-term care facilities, rehabilitation centers, community health clinics and other healthcare providers in and around Indianapolis serving some ten million patients and 20,000 physicians.

A primary service of IHIE is the Indiana Network for Patient Care (INPC), a citywide clinical network that stores and delivers laboratory, radiology, dictation, and other documents to a majority of Indianapolis office practices. It handles over 2.8 million secure health transactions daily and contains over 3 billion pieces of clinical data including 80 million radiology images, 50 million text reports and 750,000 EKG readings. Using INPC a physician can quickly see all the images a patient has had no matter where in the area covered by IHIE they were performed. [4]

IHIE has some 70 employees devoted to developing and supporting its services and the sophisticated data normalization and standardization that makes them possible. Given IHIE's success it is easy to imagine that we should have something like this in every region of the country. However, in the complex adaptive healthcare system of healthcare, it has proven formidably difficult to fund an operation like IHIE. The economic challenge is familiar. How do you get the beneficiaries of the information sharing to pay for it?

In fact, IHIE might well not exist without the support of the Regenstrief Foundation, a 25-year old research organization dedicated to the study and improvement of health and healthcare delivery. There are successful centralized HIEs in Wisconsin and a few other communities but, in general, the model has been difficult to launch and sustain. In our country which places a great premium on privacy and independence there are also "political" issues with this model. People understandably worry about who is looking at their data. A very specific concern has been that health insurance companies might see health data and deny coverage for pre-existing conditions. Assuming the new health reform bill remains in force, now that the Supreme Court has upheld it, this concern might be mitigated, since it outlaws discrimination in health insurance based on pre-existing conditions. Additionally, in many communities, health systems view HIE as a way of creating close business relationships with their referral sources and do not necessarily want to support an more inclusive approach that essentially levels the field with respect to access to clinical data.

Beyond these issues, the federated model is increasingly seen as the more sustainable HIE solution for reasons that closely parallel the economic drivers of cloud computing. Under a federated model there is generally no central data normalization or standardization. The Internet is used as the vehicle for moving data among the federated EHRs with special software performing the work necessary to transfer data in a secure, private and trusted manner.

We will now turn to discussion of some specific HIE technologies starting with DIRECT, a specific model to support federated HIE, and CONNECT, a centralized open source technology. Both are supported by ONC. After this we will look at a few commercial federated HIE technologies.

DIRECT: In March 2010 ONC launched DIRECT, a set of specifications that utilizes secure email and encrypted attachments to transport information from one EHR to another. [5] An important supporting element of DIRECT is a Health ISP (HISP), a software service that provides a special electronic provider directory that is maintained by a trusted source much as professional licensure and credentials are maintained by the relevant state board. The HISP can also distribute special "keys" necessary to encrypt and decrypt email attachments and can route DIRECT emails to their proper destination.[7]

To understand the potential of this federated approach we'll consider a hypothetical, but not unrealistic, "advanced" implementation of DIRECT. It might work like the Share button on many web pages where a user can click, and an article, photo or video is sent to a specified friend. Similarly, to send a patient summary to another physician might only require a click on a button or link. From there it would be necessary to look up the receiving physician in the HISP. Ideally, the lookup function would be integrated into the EHR. As we discussed earlier, this sort of integration of services from one web site into another is already very common on the Internet. Once the receiving physician is known, the EHR would retrieve their special DIRECT email address and their public key for use in encrypting the record as an email attachment. The record, now encrypted, would become an attachment on a secure email message. Since the email address came from the HISP, there is an assurance that the message will end up where it is supposed to go. However, permission from the patient for this information exchange must be dealt with outside of DIRECT.

The email would be sent to the DIRECT inbox of the provider to whom the patient is being referred and, ideally, the provider's EHR would retrieve the email, decrypt it using their private key and interpret the data, placing it into proper context in the patient's record. For example, lab tests or physiologic measurements from the referring provider could become part of the profiles for those values in the recipient's EHR. This last step typically requires that the attachment is in a special format we'll discuss next. This hypothetical exchange of a record using DIRECT is illustrated in Fig. 3.1. As with many of the illustrations, it intentionally avoids some technical details in the interest of clarity.

---

[7] We'll discuss encryption in more detail in the security section of this chapter but it typically involves two "digital keys" (long strings of characters). You encrypt a message to someone using their public key but you need a private key – something that only the recipient should have – to un-encrypt it. This insures that only the intended recipient can read the message.

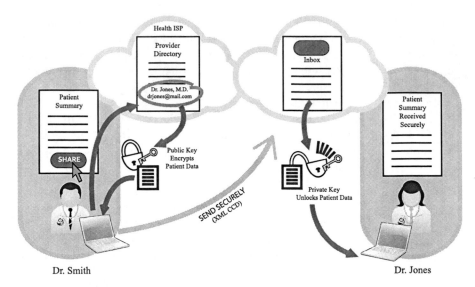

Fig. 3.1 A Simplified Representation of the Exchange of an XML Formatted Continuity of Care (CCD) Document using DIRECT

In its original conceptualization DIRECT was seen as a digital replacement for the fax machine physicians commonly use to share charts. Indeed, the DIRECT attachment can be just that – a PDF or TIFF image useful for very little other than viewing or printing at the receiving end. As we'll see in the later chapters, DIRECT can be, and is starting to be, used for far more interesting things such as the example of sharing clinical data we just gave or even sharing data from an EHR with the patient. It is important to understanding where things are going to recall that Stage 2 of Meaningful Use requires that patients actually access their data and exchange messages with their provider using "secure messaging" - DIRECT.

Rather than an image of a paper document, the attachment could be an Xtensible Markup Language (XML) formatted Continuity of Care Document (CCD), a machine readable patient summary record now accepted by the federal government as the key informational component of care coordination via health information exchange. The ability to create the CCD is part of certification, so any certified EHR can produce it. The specifics of what it contains from EHR to EHR are not as consistent as would be ideal, however, so there are a number of associated issues and concerns in merging clinical data obtained using DIRECT from disparate EHRs as we've just hypothesized. [6] We'll further explain XML and take a closer look at the CCD in the section on Data and Interoperability Standards.

CONNECT: ONC has also supported the development of CONNECT, an open source technology for the more robust kind of health information exchange that does, at least for now, require a centralized approach. [7] As we have seen, DIRECT is a simple, inexpensive way for providers to share information and, as we'll discuss in a later chapter, for patients to gain access to it. At present, it does not deal with a number of fairly complex issues that CONNECT specifically does manage.

Since it is politically impossible to have a universal health ID number in the US, and social security numbers cannot legally be used for this purpose, there is always the problem of accurately identifying patients and correctly linking their data across health organizations. CONNECT includes a *cross organizational* Master Patient Index (sometimes called an XMPI) to resolve patient identity. The term MPI (or Enterprise MPI) has typically meant an index of patients within a health system. If health information exchange encompasses multiple health systems then an MPI designed for this purpose is needed. As we discussed, in the IHIE it is possible for a provider to see all clinical data about a patient in one view, including actual medical images. CONNECT can support a similar capability by maintaining what is often called a document locator service, essentially an index to where specific data about each patient is stored. Finally, CONNECT has facilities for describing and managing institutional privacy and security policies as well as patient-specific authorization decisions with respect to access to their data.

CONNECT is free and can be downloaded by any health system or HIE. However, like all centralized health information exchange platforms, it is complex, and both installing and maintaining CONNECT requires significant technical expertise and ongoing people and technical resources. A current list of CONNECT installations is posted on the project's web site. [7]

Commercial Solutions: There are a number of commercial systems that provide tools or complete systems to support a centralized or federated model of health information exchange. The two largest providers are OptumInsight™ and Medicity. OptumInsight (formerly Axolotl) is part of a wholly owned subsidiary of UnitedHealth whose goal is to provide an integrated technology solution for the delivery of care under outcome-based contracts. Medicity, now a wholly owned subsidiary of Aetna, has similar goals. It is very significant that two of the four largest commercial health insurance companies[8] are now major providers of health informatics solutions for creating a more integrated and coordinated form of healthcare. By all appearances we have crossed an important bridge and there may be no turning back.

A number of enterprise health system software solutions now also provide their own technology for health information exchange, even if they contain third party system components such as EHRs from a competing company. Siemens, for example, acquired MobileMD™ to provide these capabilities. Cerner has partnered with Certify Data Systems to utilize its HealthDock™ described by Cerner as an "intelligent appliance that enables the secure electronic flow of clinical data between hospitals and provider offices". Its push technology sends results and clinical documents to the provider's EHR saving time spent checking to see if they are available. It can also be used to place orders.

---

[8] WellPoint and Kaiser are the others but Kaiser has a substantially different business model and would not likely consider becoming a technology supplier.

Exactly how the technology architecture of health information exchange will ultimately play out isn't clear at this point and it will be very interesting to watch it evolve over the coming years.

Privacy, Security and Trust

No health information technology is useful in the real world unless it can provide sufficient protections for who has access to what elements of each patient's data (Privacy) – assurance that only authorized persons or entities can access that data (Security), and that everyone involved can be certain that the data they are sharing is going to the person or entity they want it to go to (Trust).

Congress addressed this issue in HIPAA, reasoning that, for the health industry to adopt digital technology, there had to be a clear definition of the necessary data protections. Interestingly, the primary original motivator for the act was not improved patient care. It was helping employees keep their insurance when they changed jobs and administrative reform, the desire to introduce and have widespread adoption of new electronic formats mostly for the exchange of financial datasets such as the ANSI 837 format for claims and the ANSI 835 electronic remittance advice.

Today, with the focus now more on the automation of clinical data, HIPAA regulations are of great importance to all health providers considering electronic records. The rather complex details of HIPAA aren't important here but I can recommend one clearly written and not overly long practitioners' guide to those who are interested in them. [8] What we will focus on his *how* privacy, security and trust are supported by health informatics systems.

Privacy: Patients, by law, own their clinical records. Their provider may own the paper on which they are recorded or the disk on which they are stored but the data itself is owned by the patient. Only the patient or their personal representative can authorize exactly who can view that data and for what purposes. There are exceptions, of course. These include direct treatment (T) situations, transmitting information to get paid (P), and certain specific administrative functions necessary in the operations (O) of healthcare entities, such as accreditation, quality management, reporting to healthcare agencies for comparative analysis and internal training activities. Together these are often referred to as TPO.

Beyond these, it is generally the case that access to PHI must be limited based on the patient's preferences. This can be relatively simple in an office practice but consider what might happen with electronic records, particularly if they are connected to an HIE. A cancer patient, for example, might want to disclose certain aspects of their care to support a research effort for their particular condition or to see if they qualify for a clinical trial. They might not want to release other aspects of their care, such as a sexually transmitted disease or a mental health problem. The general principle here is referred to as "granular control" of health records (or "data segmentation" in the report that we'll quote in the following paragraphs). It has to do with how clinical data can be logically grouped for the purposes of patient consent to its use beyond TPO. This principle is yet not well implemented so developing a workable data segmentation schema is one of the initiatives of the S & I Framework collaborative, "a community of volunteers from the public and private sectors who are focused on providing the tools, services and guidance to facilitate the functional exchange of health information". [9]

This is a critical issue if clinical data is going to be used as widely as possible for purposes beyond direct patient care. According to a September, 2010 report by the George Washington University School of Public Policy, "The issue of whether and, if so, to what extent patients should have control over the sharing or withholding of their health information represents one of the foremost policy challenges related to electronic health information exchange." [10]

This report goes on to say that "The ability to segment information within an EHR and, more broadly, in the context of electronic exchange, largely depends (from a technical feasibility standpoint) on a number of factors, including the ability to capture information in structured data fields, the application of common data definitions and terminologies so that such information can be interpreted correctly by others, and the use of common standards for sharing the information." This is, in essence, the problem of data interoperability which we'll come to in the next section.

First, we need to focus on the consumer. There is "near universal agreement in all the groups that, if medical data are to be stored electronically, healthcare consumers should have some say in how those data are shared and used." [11]

This raises at least two important and largely unresolved issues. The first is the mechanism for consumer engagement. "Exercising individual preferences for information sharing (i.e., making segmentation decisions) presumes a level of understanding about what is possible, what is desirable, and what the potential consequences of those decisions may be. Packed into this process are some very real concerns about the capacity of individuals to appreciate these nuances and act accordingly, as well as more logistical concerns about how individuals could reasonably be expected to articulate their preferences in a manner that could be honored by multiple, diverse data holders in the healthcare environment." [10]

Beyond this is the difficult informatics challenge of exactly how these preferences are to be expressed by the consumer. Given the multiple stakeholders potentially interested in health data, one could envision a whole series of questions or preferences attached to each and every data item in an electronic record. Will consumers be able to understand and operate such a mechanism? Will they be willing to devote the time it takes? If not, will health data in practical terms not be shareable in practical terms outside of the TPO situations?

Researchers at Georgia Tech's Information and Security Center (GTISC) are interested in these problems and have developed MedVault, a system for secure and privacy-preserving storage of health information one component of which is an easy-to-understand patient-facing tool (Fig. 3.2) that simplifies the issues into a familiar "Who, What, How and When" set of options. [12]

Of these, "What" is the most complex to implement in a usable way. Answering even these simple questions for every granular element in their chart would require a great deal of the patient's time. Moreover, in many cases, patients would be dealing

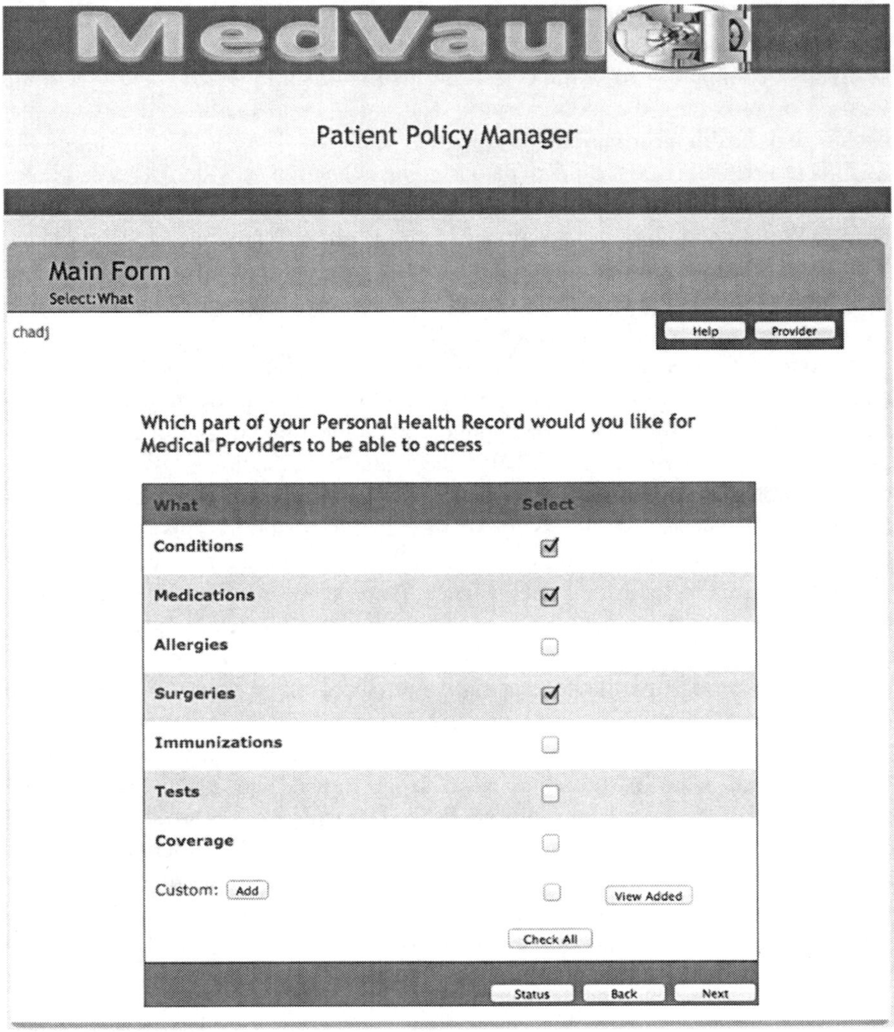

Fig. 3.2 MedVault Provides a User Friendly Tool for Patients to Express their Privacy Choices

with unfamiliar technical terms. One of the goals of the data segmentation effort is to define the "granules" at a workable level that could be understood by most patients. Another difficult issue is properly linking the defined granules to the multiplicity of health data elements that might be in a chart.

There is a second issue, "how should the needs of individual patients be considered relative to those of various other stakeholders who may desire access to the information in question and/or prefer not to confront the practical and logistical implications of distinguishing it from other non-sensitive information." [10] Information about certain communicable diseases is already shared with public health officials without specific patient consent. What are the over-riding societal needs in this regard?

Security: Privacy is about what persons or entities have legitimate access to PHI. Security is about preventing unauthorized access. It's a highly technical topic so we will only discuss it at a high level here.

Data breaches most often come about because an employee with legitimate access either cooperates with someone who wants unauthorized access or innocently does something that provides such access. A recent incident in a metro Atlanta hospital caused it to turn away patients for a few days because of "malware" (a virus or other software program designed to disrupt computers or steal data) infecting its computers and data network. It is likely that an employee introduced the malware by bringing an infected USB flash drive (USB memory stick) to work. Once present in a networked computer system, malware can spread rapidly and can damage data files or even transmit sensitive information to computers outside that network, making such information available to the creators of the malware. Most commonly the target of the creators is information that can be converted into money, such as credit card information or information that could be used to create fraudulent healthcare claims. A well-publicized incident of this type occurred in Florida where an employee of the Cleveland Clinic sold PHI for 1,100 patients to her cousin who owned a medical claims processing business and used the data to generate millions of dollars in fraudulent claims. [13] A different but also high profile incident involved curious hospital employees looking at the records of a number of celebrities. [14]

Another potential source of concern, particularly in healthcare, is the loss or theft of mobile computing devices. Incidents of this kind are often reported in the press when they occur. [15] Mobile devices should be protected by strong passwords that are changed at a reasonably frequent interval. Moreover, the data on the disks in these devices should be encrypted so that even a thief who can get around the password protection cannot access the data.

A third area of concern is the movement of PHI over networks, particularly the Internet. Here encryption is not optional. The Internet was not designed with security in mind. It was originally used by only a few national research laboratories that knew and trusted each other.

The importance of encryption of PHI is highlighted by the new trends in health information exchange, such as DIRECT. In the following chapters we'll see that cloud-based tools for data transport are increasingly being used in clinical practice particularly outside of the hospital. These trends only amplify the need for routine use of encryption to assure data is not compromised.

So, what exactly is encryption? This is a highly mathematical subject and anything beyond a very basic conceptual explanation is outside the scope of this book. [16] In healthcare information exchange we are primarily concerned with a kind of encryption called public key encryption. The central idea is that two very large numbers are generated in a way that they are mathematically related, but determining one from the other is prohibitively time consuming and expensive. The end products are a "public key" that can be made available to everyone that an individual or business wants to securely share information with and a "private key" that, importantly, only that individual or business has access to.

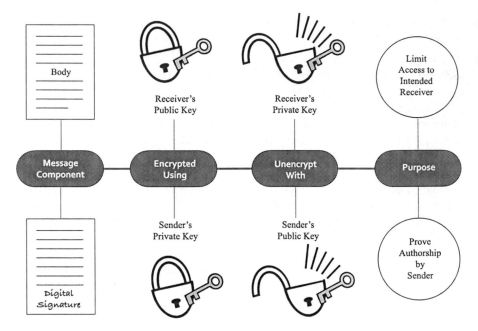

Fig. 3.3 A Simplified Illustration of Public Key Encryption

Given these keys, two things can be accomplished. First, the protected health information can be secured so only the intended recipient can view it. This is because a message encrypted ("scrambled") with the *intended recipient's public key* cannot be decrypted ("unscrambled") by anyone unless they possess the matching private key so, presumably, *only the intended recipient* can open it. It is important to note that compromise of the recipient's private key defeats this. This could happen if malware infected a computer where the key is stored and stole it.

Trust: In addition to encrypting the data so only the intended recipient can read it, public key encryption can help make sure that the person who sent the message is who they say they are. This is done by also sending a "digital signature", an associated message encrypted with the *sender's private key*. Assuming only the sender has this private key, then when anyone opens the digital signature using the *sender's public key* they have proof of who sent the message.

Fig. 3.3 summarizes the two important capabilities of Public Key Encryption we just discussed. As with many of the illustrations, it intentionally avoids some technical details in the interest of clarity. For example, in a health system, a more complex infrastructure might well be in place.

An associated issue is how to make certain that a public key is correct and belongs to the claimed person or entity. The usual solution is a public-key infrastructure (PKI), in which one or more third parties, known as certificate authorities, certify ownership of key pairs. PKI allows entities to trust that the public key they are using does actually belong to who it is claimed to belong to. The certificate binds the public key to an entity, and that binding is certified by the authority. This adds complexity and cost but it is widely used because no fully satisfactory alternate solution to the public key authentication problem is known.

There is also the issue of making sure data is being routed to where it is intended to go. Each provider in a DIRECT HIE also has a special email address for use only in sending DIRECT messages. A process will be put into place to make sure that each person or entity has a legitimate right to exchange PHI and that the address is issued to the correct person or entity. The HISP will provide a related service so that any provider in the HIE can look up the trusted DIRECT email address of any other provider. HISPs can talk to other HISPs so, as DIRECT expands, this lookup service and the ability to send DIRECT messages may become available regionally, state-wide or even nationally.

Of course, the centralized HIE technologies also have a provider directory service to manage trust. In these technologies DIRECT messages aren't being sent, so this directory information is not in the form of an email address but, like a hospital's credentialing system, it is designed to make sure that everyone can have faith that data is being shared with the correct entity.

Most vendors of HIE technology now provide the necessary tools for DIRECT, including HISP software. Anyone can create a DIRECT exchange. As a result, most health systems that have an HIE will likely soon offer or are already offering DIRECT and operate their own HISP. In all cases, the HISP will need to be maintained by a trusted entity. This might be the health system or, in a cross enterprise HIE it might be a state designated agency. Whoever it is will probably mange the PKI infrastructure for providers within their HIE. A process will be put into place to make certain that everyone is who they claim to be and that the certificates are correctly issued to the person or entity that has a legitimate right to use them. Outside of a health system the HISP and the entity that operates it may also operate the PKI infrastructure.

Interoperability

In general we are considering health informatics from the provider practice perspective. In this section we'll take a brief detour into the world of hospital information systems in order to discuss another long term goal of the field: interoperability. Interoperability is the ability of diverse systems and organizations to work together and exchange data meaningfully. It should already be clear that here in the US we have a very diverse set of health information systems implemented in our hospitals and clinics. In fact most US health systems have a very diverse set of information systems *within their own enterprise* so interoperability is not just an issue across health systems.

In countries with a single payer health system it is feasible, but not certain, that a single EHR or a small group of EHRs along with a national HIE would be provided, paid for by the system and used by all providers. [17] Almost by definition, this solves much of the interoperability issue. Arguably the best example of this single-system approach in the US is the Veteran's Administration (VA) that has a system wide EHR called VistA (Veterans Health Information System and Technology Architecture).

The early history of VistA is a fascinating health informatics story and one in which I was peripherally involved back in the early 1970's. The late Joseph T. "Ted" O'Neill and a small group of "co-conspirators" hatched a plan in Ted's living room to infiltrate the VA and launch the open-source development of a system wide EHR based on MUMPS (Massachusetts General Hospital Utility Multi-Programming System), a technology developed in the late 1960's to facilitate the development of clinical information systems.

Incredibly and against very long odds, the plan eventually worked and today the VA has a single system-wide EHR. The results can be impressive. For example, a VA physician can, with a few mouse clicks, call up any images or other clinical data relevant to their patient from *anywhere* in the nationwide VA system.

Of course this requires agreement or a mandate that everyone will use the same systems. There is a long history of this issue playing out in US hospitals and across the health informatics industry. Today a few companies dominate the large scale enterprise health information system business. Listed in order of their founding or the founding date of their oldest component, they are: Siemens (1968 as Shared Medical Systems), MEDITECH (1969), Allscripts (1971 as Technicon Data Systems), McKesson (1974 as HBO & Co), Cerner (1979) and EPIC (1979). To automate virtually all aspects of a larger hospital or health system (no vendor can do them all) these companies represent the available options. There are a few others that specialize mostly in small hospitals.

Early on there were no vendors that could automate an entire hospital. SMS began by offering hospital financial management systems. Two of today's market leaders, EPIC and MEDITECH (both MUMPS-based), began, respectively, as suppliers of EMR and laboratory information systems. Cerner also began as a supplier of laboratory information systems. Two other vendors started with fairly advanced system concepts. HBO & Co began with a patient information system called MedPro. Technicon Data Systems began as a Lockheed effort in the mid-1960's to commercialize technology developed in the space program by creating a very early clinical information system at El Camino Hospital in California.

Each of these companies attempted to expand from their initial base by offering more and more subsystems with the goal of being a sole source health informatics provider to health enterprises. Initially virtually all spending was on financial and administrative systems. The exception was laboratory and pharmacy automation that were a particular focus because these departments were major revenue generators. Radiology would join them as modern imaging came into its own and computers became capable of storing images digitally. By the late 1980's a quarter of spending was on systems in support of patient care. [18]

However, it was difficult to have sufficient expertise in all areas, so "specialty vendors" emerged with a deep focus in particular areas. As a result, hospitals often ended up with a number of systems specialized for specific departments. Steve Rushing, long time health IT consultant and now my Georgia Tech colleague, never fails to mention the politics of health informatics. In this case he points out that the organizational structure of the institution and the incentives for the executives were usually based on the performance of individual divisions or departments, and this has been, and remains, a major contributing factor to shaping solution choices. As a result, there was less demand for a hospital-wide solution in the early days and, in some institutions, this is still the case. However, no matter what, solutions were needed to key hospital-wide functions such as charge data capture and order entry/ results reporting.

This led to the development of a standards movement for data sharing and the concept of an Open Systems Interconnection (OSI) model as well as the first HL7 proposal. HL7 is the main international healthcare informatics interoperability standards organization. Its name derives from the seventh and final layer of the OSI Reference model – the application layer. This is where the sharing of administrative, financial and clinical data occurs.

In 1984 Don Simborg, one of the HL7 co-founders, created Simborg Systems. He describes its StatLAN as "the first network-based patient care system for hospitals and the basis for the founding of HL7." In essence a great battle had begun. Should hospitals seek one integrated single-vendor solution or should they procure the "best of breed" and use an "integration engine" to tie them together into the equivalent of a single integrated solution?

Today that issue is largely, but certainly not entirely, resolved in favor of a single vendor integrated solution for at least two reasons. First, the major hospital information system companies have grown to a size and scale that they can now provide the vast majority of the functional requirements of a health system. Second, as payment models shift in ways that place real economic value on care quality and efficiency, meaningful *clinical* integration is increasingly seen as strategic to a health system's success. This requires interoperability at the data level, something that is very hard to achieve using a "best of breed" approach in which each vendor made its own decisions about data element definitions.

As we discussed earlier, the management of chronic disease very typically involves many practice locations across a community or regional area. One solution to this problem is for all locations to have a common EHR. Some aggressive health systems are trying to accomplish this, often by buying the key practices in their area or by providing or subsidizing EHR systems for practices in their area that send them substantial referrals. Absent such a broadly implemented single vendor solution, many health systems are now sponsoring an HIE to accomplish the same goal of making it easy for local providers to do business with them. However, in any environment where multiple EHR systems are deployed, interoperability remains a key issue for integration of care. Some degree of standardization may always be required to fully solve this problem.

Data and Interoperability Standards

In general terms there are two important classes of standards for health data. **Data Standards** deal with how *the data itself* is classified and described. For example, is it "hypertension" or "high blood pressure"? Do we describe the serum potassium value in *mEq* or *mmol*? While these differences can often be bridged using technology, this adds to the cost and complexity of information systems and is never perfect. **Interoperability Standards** deal with *how data is packaged* into electronic documents such as a discharge summary, medication profile and so on. Standard packaging is important so that these documents can be easily exchanged and understood among EHR systems for purposes like data aggregation for quality reporting or monitoring public health.

Data Standards[9]: In the early days computers were far too slow to process free text into something useful. Storage space was very expensive and limited. Virtually everyone felt that the answer was to capture and store highly structured information so that ambiguities were eliminated, or at least greatly reduced, and the computers of the day would have something they could store and process in a reasonable time frame at an affordable cost.

The problem has long been that entering structured data is usually more time consuming for the provider than dictating free text (basically the way we humans express ourselves). As we'll see in Chapter 4, modern computers are up to the job of Natural Language Processing (NLP) in order to turn unstructured free text dictation into SNOMED, the most comprehensive, structured clinical nomenclature available. So, to some extent, it's now a moot point. In theory there is no reason why providers cannot keep doing what they often prefer to do which is to dictate or type notes and the computer will do the rest. However, as of now, NLP technologies are well integrated into only a few EHRs.

Every provider is already familiar with the concept of data standards, largely because of billing. Diagnoses *must* be coded into the International Classification of Disease (ICD) and procedures into Current Procedural Terminology (CPT) for providers to be paid.

There are two main reasons. The first is to force providers to be precise about what they mean. This is essential for accurate reimbursement. It is also highly desirable so that insurance companies can try to avoid fraud through duplicate claims. It also helps avoid errors through miscommunication and misinterpretation of clinical data. Larry Weed was early to recognize this with respect to medical records. He argued that providers need to unambiguously state the patient's problems, the reason why they feel they are problems and their plan for dealing with each problem. In his early attempts to create a computer based record virtually all data entry was

---

[9] There are many health data standards. I've listed the major ones in the glossary and have chosen to use SNOMED as the example because it is the most clinically powerful. The Glossary contains the names, acronyms and a brief description of the commonly used standards.

from predefined lists to force what he considered the necessary level of precision. This approach was not popular with his house staff, whom I spoke with, because it took more time than traditional charting, a problem that, as we've said, is still largely unresolved today.

The second reason is because computer systems in use for purposes such as claims processing were usually written years ago and were designed to handle structured and consistent terminology. Humans, on the other hand, are remarkably adept at free text. We deal with ambiguity and the context sensitivity of word meanings without even thinking about it. For example, consider these phrases: "I swatted the fly" and "I hit a fly ball". The word "fly" has entirely different meanings which we understand subconsciously because the context sensitivity of language is apparently wired into our brains. Until relatively recently computers were not particularly good at this. IBM's Watson, the winner of the popular game show *Jeopardy*, against expert human competition, is evidence of how far the technology has come. The first commercial application of Watson may be to answer questions posed by physicians at the point-of-care. [19]

Getting paid for clinical services is important, so everyone pays close attention to assigning the correct ICD and CPT codes to the billing records for each patient encounter. For the same reason National Drug Codes (NDC) are assigned to medications by pharmacies and Logical Observation Identifiers Names and Codes (LOINC) are assigned to laboratory studies. These codes are all widely used, but they have each typically been a list of terms for their domain of interest. While they certainly add more precision to medical and billing records, they each only encompass a part of the complete health domain; they don't code in great detail so they may artificially group what are not necessarily identical patients; and they don't express clinical relationships so that, for example, a computer with only these codes may not be able to easily search for any patient who has had their left thumb amputated rather than just patients who have had an amputation.

That is because, for the most part, we have not applied the same level of precision to the information we code as we do when we record it in charts. Doing this will require a different approach. The current transition from ICD-9 to ICD-10 is, in large part, about introducing this extra precision. [20]

The earliest attempt to introduce significant structure into coding of medical data may have been the Standardized Nomenclature of Pathology (SNOP) begun in 1965 by Dr. Arnold W Pratt at the National Institutes of Health (NIH). Dr. Pratt's vision was that computers could "read" free text and convert it into a hierarchical structured language. The terms would be standardized and the hierarchy would represent clinical relationships so that, for example, the computer would "know" that the ulna is a bone in the arm or that glomerulonephritis is an inflammatory disease of the kidney. The end goal was to use routinely collected clinical data to support research and other purposes beyond patient care. Today we call that "secondary use" of clinical data and it is still one of the objectives of the national effort to deploy health information technology.

Later on, under the leadership of two other pathologists, Dr. Roger Cote at the University of Sherbrooke and Dr. David J. Rothwell at the Medical College of Wisconsin, the concept was expanded to the Standardized Nomenclature of Medicine

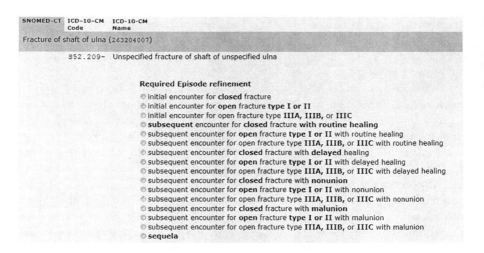

SNOMED-CT	ICD-10-CM Code	ICD-10-CM Name
Fracture of shaft of ulna (263204007)		
	S52.209-	Unspecified fracture of shaft of unspecified ulna

Required Episode refinement

- initial encounter for **closed** fracture
- initial encounter for **open** fracture **type I or II**
- initial encounter for open fracture type **IIIA, IIIB, or IIIC**
- **subsequent** encounter for **closed** fracture **with routine healing**
- subsequent encounter for **open** fracture **type I or II** with routine healing
- subsequent encounter for open fracture type **IIIA, IIIB, or IIIC** with routine healing
- subsequent encounter for **closed** fracture with **delayed** healing
- subsequent encounter for **open** fracture **type I or II** with delayed healing
- subsequent encounter for open fracture type **IIIA, IIIB, or IIIC** with delayed healing
- subsequent encounter for **closed** fracture with **nonunion**
- subsequent encounter for **open** fracture **type I or II** with nonunion
- subsequent encounter for open fracture type **IIIA, IIIB, or IIIC** with nonunion
- subsequent encounter for **closed** fracture with **malunion**
- subsequent encounter for **open** fracture **type I or II** with malunion
- subsequent encounter for open fracture type **IIIA, IIIB, or IIIC** with malunion
- **sequela**

Fig. 3.4 An Example of Mapping between ICD-10 and SNOMED

(SNOMED). Today, SNOMED CT, the clinical terminology subset of SNOMED, is a standard accepted by the US government and is increasingly seen as a key tool for the advancement of clinical health informatics. ICD-10 has many similar hierarchical structures and a mapping between it and SNOMED CT has been developed. [21] There is talk of merging the two into a single common international standard, something that will probably happen in the future.

As shown in Fig. 3.4, ICD-10 requires additional specification that might affect reimbursement. SNOMED is more focused on describing clinical detail. In fact, SNOMED CT "understands" that the operative morphology of "fracture of shaft of ulna" is a fracture and that the shaft is a part of the Ulna. These are intentionally simple examples to give you a feel for the information that is contained in the hierarchical structure and the more generalized research and clinical decision support capabilities that it could support. That is best appreciated by using an online SNOMED-CT browser. [22] I encourage readers with a serious interest in the topic to do this.

Interoperability Standards: Whether the data is structured or free text it should ideally be wrapped for transport in some standard electronic document format so that a computer understands what each section of the data is and what it represents (i.e. where the lab results and the medication orders are and how they have been coded). This format has been standardized. The HL7 Clinical Document Architecture (CDA) uses XML for encoding of the structure of the documents, but not their informational contents, dividing the document into generic, unnamed, and sections without a defined template. Stated another way, CDA is an XML-based markup standard intended to specify the encoding, structure and semantics of *clinical documents* for health information exchange but it does not specify the format of the contents of these documents.

Extensible Markup Language (XML) is used in virtually all domains to which computing is applied. It defines a set of rules for encoding documents in a format

Problems

Condition	Condition Status
AV Nodal Reentry Tachycardia	Resolved
Lyme Disease	Resolved
Low HDL Cholesterol	Resolved
Corneal Abrasion	Resolved
Vegan	Active

Fig. 3.5 Simple Human Readable Display of Part of a Continuity of Care Document (CCD)

that is both human-readable[10] and machine-readable. Its key tool is tags with standard names that tell the computer what data they enclose. We'll see an example of these tags in a moment. Fig. 3.5 is a very simple example of how an XML document might be visualized for a human to read. It is taken from a CCD posted on the Internet by Dr. John Halamka, the CIO of a leading Boston hospital. [23] I recommend his blog, *Life as a Healthcare CIO*. [24]

So CDA specifies the structure of the documents, but what about their contents? A number of key documents have been defined by the Healthcare Information Technology Standards Panel (HITSP). They are the C28 – Emergency Care Summary Document, C32 – Summary Documents Using CCD, C35 – Lab Result Terminology, C38 – Patient Level Quality Data Document, C72 – Immunization Message and the C78 – Immunization Document. More globally the modules that might be used in any of these documents comprise the C83 CDA Content Modules standard. [25] For our purposes it is only necessary to know that these standards go into an incredible amount of detail.

For now let's focus on the key CDA document for care coordination, the CCD. You can think of it as a digital version of the cover sheet or clinical summary typical of paper charts. It would likely contain the patient's key demographic data, problem list, medications, allergies, laboratory results and so on. As opposed to a paper version, this data is both digital, so a computer can read it, and it is "tagged" using XML so a computer knows what each item of data is. A CCD can be quite complex but the basic concept is easy to understand.

On the following page I provide part of the vital signs from the XML taken from a sample CCD posted by the HIMSS Electronic Health Record Association. [26][11]

I've highlighted three codes that are important to computer interpretation of what follows. The first:

```
<templateId root="2.16.840.1.113883.10.20.1.16"/>
```

tells the computer what template to use for this information. A template basically defines the sections that should be present. The second:

---

[10] However, a human would not want to sit down and read an XML document as one would read a book. The problem of visualizing the information in an XML document most usefully for humans is still an area of active research and development.

[11] The technically inclined might go to reference 26 and click the *Download the CCD QSG* (Quick Start Guide) link. It provides two full CCD examples and a guide to study.

```
codeSystem="2.16.840.1.113883.6.1"
```
tells the computer that the coding system used is LOINC, one of the systems we mentioned under Data Standards.

Sample of XML from a CCD[12]:

```
<templateId root="2.16.840.1.113883.10.20.1.16"/>
<!- Vital signs section template ->
<code code="8716-3" codeSystem="2.16.840.1.113883.6.1"/>
<title>Vital Signs</title>
<thead><tr>
<th align="right">Date / Time: </th>
 <th>Nov 14, 1999</th>
 <th>April 7, 2000</th>
</tr></thead>
<tbody><tr>
<th align="left">Blood Pressure</th>
 <td>132/86 mmHg</td>
 <td>145/88 mmHg</td>
</tr></tbody>
```

Technically inclined readers will notice that this illustration, taken from a web page, has some HTML tags mixed in with the XML. They are for formatting of the web page for human viewing and are not needed for machine interpretation of the XML.
The third:
```
code code="8716-3"
```
is the LOINC code for vital signs. You have had your vital signs taken if you have ever had a medical office visit. Vital signs normally include height, weight, temperature and blood pressure. I only show blood pressure and I removed some of the HTML tags to save space. I also reformatted the sample to prevent lines from wrapping over to make it easier to read. To test your understanding of this sample and to verify that XML is reasonably human readable, you should easily be able to figure out that this patient has two blood pressure readings and that the second of these was higher than the first. See if you can verify that by studying the **Sample of XML from a CCD (above)**.

This brief introduction to XML and the CCD should give you a sense of what is possible. Since a computer can read the clinical information and use the coding system information to "understand" what it means then a CCD sent from one provider's office to another could, in theory, be broken up into the individual data items by the receiving provider's certified EHR and put into the patient's record, as we described earlier.

---

[12] We've not previously discussed a predecessor of the CCD, the CCR, because the CCD has been accepted as the US standard format for an electronic patient summary. At present an EHR can be certified if it can generate either the CCD or CCR format but the trend is in the direction of the CCD. The differences are quite technical [26] but, most importantly, the CCD was developed within the CDA architecture.

The exchange of these electronic documents shows the potential of information technology to transform and expedite processes. Today, in most offices, the process of sending clinical data for purposes of a patient referral would involve pulling a paper chart, making a copy and either faxing that copy or mailing it to the office to which the patient is being referred. The referring office would then reverse the process. This involves costly and error prone manual processing at both ends. Moreover, the information is in a form that is basically useful only for reading.

The digital process, at least using DIRECT, is essentially free and virtually error proof. Moreover, the information, once received, can be combined with other digital clinical information to help the receiving physician make correct, safe and appropriate clinical decisions.

The applications of this technology aren't limited to provider referrals. Some commercial systems already use a variation on this approach to support care coordination across practices, the management of populations of chronic disease patients, and the delivery of care against quality metrics across an entire health system. We will see some examples of this in Chapter 5.

Beyond Data and Interoperability

Even the most sophisticated coding systems don't deal with the issue of the "clinical logic" – relationships among data elements or linking those relationships to current medical knowledge. For example, a chronic disease patient might have 6 problems coded in ICD-9, they might be on 12 medications and they might have recently had 10 laboratory tests and 3 imaging studies done. No existing coding system provides specific support to indicate what medications, laboratory tests and imaging studies were done for each of the patient's problems and why they were done.

As we've said, Larry Weed's solution is that the provider should specifically indicate these relationships as part of charting. His Problem Oriented Medical Record (POMR) uses the acronym SOAP to indicate this. The provider should indicate the Subjective and Objective data supporting each Assessment (problem). They should also indicate the Plan for dealing with that problem. In a computerized version of a SOAP record these relationships might then be explicit. Realistically, however, that is not terribly common. An underlying informatics structure that can infer these links is probably needed.

For the past few decades Dr. Weed has been working on his own approach to linking medical knowledge to structured records which he calls Problem-Knowledge Couplers. [27] Obviously this is greatly facilitated if the underlying medical data is coded and if the clinical relationships are explicit. Achieving this, without reducing physician productivity, is a long standing problem.

Another issue is standards of care. Ideally complex research that reveals best medical practices should itself be described in some standard form so all EHRs could more easily use it. Work supported by IBM over many years at Columbia University developed such a framework, the Arden syntax. [28] It is an artificial intelligence (AI) frame-based grammar for representing and processing medical conditions and recommendations as "Medical Logic Modules (MLMs)" for use in clinical decision support programs. Clinical decision support is the function of advanced EMRs to give physicians advice on the best management of their particular patient. It will likely be a requirement for Stage 3 of Meaningful Use. Arden syntax is now formally a standard as part of HL7. Three enterprise health system vendors[13] have implemented Arden-compliant decision support modules. It is also used by the Indiana Health Information Exchange to deliver clinical reminders to physicians but has otherwise not achieved widespread acceptance. That could change as EHR deployment spreads and the bar for Meaningful Use is raised.

Before moving on, this chapter has covered a lot of material and, on its own, could easily be expanded into an entire book. For the non-technical reader who may feel overwhelmed at this point, what is important is to have a sense of the capabilities and protections these technologies provide so that the systems we will discuss in the remaining chapters could have been developed and can function in an acceptable and legal manner.

I would encourage the more technically inclined reader to use the references to explore further those technologies of interest. There are many more web sites and publications I could have cited. There are many organizations involved in data and interoperability standards and in data privacy, security and trust. This is a very rich field that will amply reward those with the interest and expertise to spend time further exploring it.

References

1. Licklider JCR (1963) Memorandum for Members and Affiliates of the Intergalactic Computer Network   http://www.kurzweilai.net/memorandum-for-members-and-affiliates-of-the-intergalactic-computer-network. Accessed 19 July, 2012
2. http://www.meddserve.com/ Accessed 19 July, 2012
3. http://www.exleaz.com/ Accessed 19 July, 2012
4. McDonald CJ, et al (2005) The Indiana Network For Patient Care: A Working Local Health Information Infrastructure. Health Aff 24:5 1214–1220
5. http://wiki.directproject.org/ Accessed 19 July, 2012
6. Brull R (2012) Six Questions to Consider About Merging a CCD http://www.hl7standards.com/blog/2012/01/24/merging-a-ccd/ Accessed 19 July, 2012
7. http://www.connectopensource.org/ Accessed 19 July, 2012
8. http://www.stanford.edu/group/psylawseminar/HIPAAguide.htm Accessed 19 July, 2012
9. http://wiki.siframework.org/Data%2B;Segmentation%2B;for%2B;Privacy%2B;Homepage Accessed 19 July, 2012
10. Goldstein MM and Rein AL (2010) Data Segmentation in Electronic Health Information Exchange: Policy Considerations and Analysis http://healthit.hhs.gov/portal/server.pt?open=512%26;mode=2%26;cached=true%26;objID=1147 Accessed 19 July, 2012

---

[13] Eclypsis, now part of Allscripts, McKesson Provider Technologies and Siemens

11. Schneider S et al (2009) Consumer Engagement in Developing Electronic Health Information Systems. Prepared for: Agency for Health Research and Quality. AHRQ Pub No. 09-0018-EF
12. Mohan A, Bauer D, Blough DM, Ahamad M, et al (2009) A Patient-centric, Attribute-based, Source-verifiable Framework for Health Record Sharing. GIT CERCS Technical Report No. GIT-CERCS-09-11
13. http://www.hipaasolutions.org/news/US%20Attorney%20Charges%20Two%20With%20HIPAA%20Violations.pdf Accessed 19 July, 2012
14. http://articles.latimes.com/2008/aug/05/local/me-health5 Accessed 19 July, 2012
15. http://www.courierpress.com/news/2006/nov/25/women-alerted-to-id-theft-risk/?print=1 Accessed 19 July, 2012
16. Kaliski B The Mathematics of the RSA Public-Key Cryptosystem http://mathaware.org/mam/06/Kaliski.pdf Accessed 19 July, 2012
17. Gray BH et al (2011) Electronic Health Records: An International Perspective on "Meaningful Use" http://www.commonwealthfund.org/~/media/Files/Publications/Issue%20Brief/2011/Nov/1565_Gray_electronic_med_records_meaningful_use_intl_brief.pdf Accessed 19 July, 2012
18. Dorenfest SI (1989) The Decade of the 1980's: Large Expenditures Produce Limited Progress in Hospital Automation. US Healthc 6(12):20–2.
19. Yuan MJ (2011) Watson and healthcare: How natural language processing and semantic search could revolutionize clinical decision support. http://www.ibm.com/developerworks/industry/library/ind-watson/ Accessed 19 July, 2012
20. http://www.cms.gov/Medicare/Coding/ICD10/index.html?redirect=/ICD10/ Accessed 19 July, 2012
21. http://imagic.nlm.nih.gov/imagic/code/map Accessed 19 July, 2012
22. http://vtsl.vetmed.vt.edu/ Accessed 23 September, 2012
23. http://services.bidmc.org/geekdoctor/johnhalamkaccddocument.xml Accessed 19 July, 2012
24. http://geekdoctor.blogspot.com/ Accessed 19 July, 2012
25. http://www.hitsp.org/ConstructSet_Details.aspx?&PrefixAlpha=4&PrefixNumeric=83 Accessed 19 July, 2012
26. http://www.himssehra.org/ASP/CCD_QSG_20071112.asp Accessed 19 July, 2012
27. http://publicaa.ansi.org/sites/apdl/hitspadmin/Matrices/HITSP_09_N_451.pdf Accessed 19 July, 2012
28. Weed LL (1987) Problem-knowledge Coupling. Med Instrum. 21(5):284–7
29. Pryor TA and Hripcsak G (1993) The Arden Syntax for Medical Logic Modules. Int J Clin Monit Comput. 10(4):215–24

Chapter 4
Clinical Practice

In this chapter we'll see how the technical concepts discussed in Chapter 3 can be combined into a workable electronic health record system in the typical provider practice. I'll use as examples some systems I consider to have state-of-the-art approaches to electronic records. As we discussed in Chapter 2, there are around 1,000 commercial electronic health record systems and I'm certainly not familiar with the substantial majority of them. I have selected carefully but that doesn't mean that the systems I profile are the only – or even the best – products available, nor can I promise that they will be the best choice for any particular provider office.

Why Electronic Records?

Care Coordination: This is so obvious that it's often overlooked. Paper records are physical objects that can be in only one place at a time. They can be copied, mailed and faxed but these are not efficient processes and the records are often not available when needed at a remote location. Electronic records, when connected to a health information exchange, can be immediately available when and where needed, assuming proper procedures are in place to protect their confidentiality and to assure they are only being accessed by authorized personnel.

Safety: Paper records can also be hard to read. In its 1999 report *To Err is Human: Building a Safer Health System* the IOM estimated that avoidable medical errors contributed annually to 44,000—98,000 deaths in US hospitals. [1] Hospital-based errors were reported as the eighth leading cause of death nationwide, ahead of breast cancer, AIDS, and motor-vehicle accidents. These findings have received wide attention in the mass media as well as in medical publications. In the April 2011 issue of *Health Affairs* David Classen *et al* report that as many as one in three patients in the US encounters a medical error during a hospital stay. [2] The Agency for Health Quality and Research (AHRQ) even posts a tip sheet to help patients avoid medical errors when in the hospital. [3]

M.L. Braunstein, *Health Informatics in the Cloud*, SpringerBriefs in Computer Science, DOI 10.1007/978-1-4614-5629-2_4, © The Author(s) 2013

Among the most common and widely studied sources of error derives from medication administration. According to The Commonwealth Fund the three leading causes of medication error are performance deficit (failure to act in accordance with education and training), failure to follow a procedure or protocol, and inaccurate or omitted transcription. [4]

Improved Processes: Remember that a key issue for the effective use of information technology is to improve business processes. Ideally, process improvement should be at the top of the reasons why electronic records are deployed. In practice, this is usually not the case. The reasons relate to a lack of focus on process improvement in the project planning and design, the design of the systems themselves and the way they are implemented. Most systems are built around discrete transactions that take place within a department or working group. Even though these may be part of an overall business process that cuts across many or most of these groups, the overall process is rarely built into EHR systems. Similarly, systems are often procured and implemented without clear consideration of the overall business and its processes. As a result, each workgroup or department may well optimize things for their needs but the overall interests of the business may not be well recognized or effectively served. This is a major reason why one of the leading concerns given about adopting electronic records in the 2008 DesRoches physician EHR adoption survey [5] was the lack of any clear return on investment and decreased productivity.

Clinical Decision Support: When Larry Weed first proposed his structured medical record his goal was to help physicians organize their work. [6] For the past few decades his focus has shifted to what we now call "clinical decision support". In the early 1990s, a group of clinicians and epidemiologists at McMaster University in Ontario officially coined the term "evidence-based medicine." Here again, there are significant potential benefits from well structured clinical data or from systems that can have deep interactions with providers based on free text. Such a computer system can suggest the appropriate medical evidence and the recommended best treatment in any clinical situation. The core idea is that treatments that are shown to work should be prescribed while those that have not been proven of benefit should be avoided. With the national focus on healthcare costs this concept, once strictly the domain of medical science, has become a topic for public, and sometimes even political, discussion and debate. [7]

In *Crossing the Quality Chasm* the IOM makes wider use of evidence-based medicine a top priority. "Scientific knowledge about best care is not applied systematically or expeditiously to clinical practice. It now takes an average of 17 years for new knowledge generated by randomized controlled trails to be incorporated into practice, and even then application is highly uneven. The committee [that authored the report] therefore recommends that the Department of Health and Human Services establish a comprehensive program aimed at making scientific evidence more useful and more accessible to clinicians and patients." [8]

Improved Care Management: Better management of chronic disease is arguably the major challenge facing the health system. Among the specific issues are the traditional "one patient at a time and only when they are physically in the office" approach to care and not consistently caring for patients according to best clinical practice guidelines. Electronic records, particularly when connected via a health information exchange, can help contribute new and key tools to clinical practice to facilitate care outside of the clinic and to use the best, most up to date treatments.

Data from connected EHRs can be brought together to build a registry – an aggregated database of actionable health information across a practice or a group of affiliated practices. There the data is most frequently used to identify patients whose care is not consistent with clinical guidelines and/or the outcomes required to earn incentive payments under one form or another of pay-for-performance. It is possible to create and manage a registry as a stand-alone system independent of an electronic health record and even where no EHR is used. There are commercial products designed to do this by mining the needed data from claims, health information exchanges, laboratory test records and other sources. Registry functionality can also be built into an electronic health record system, so population health management, the key goal of a registry, is among potential EHR benefits. Over time, I believe more and more EHR systems will offer this functionality. However, there are clearly issues with population health management when multiple electronic record systems are involved across multiple practices. We'll discuss this in more detail and look at a registry system in the next chapter.

Clinical reminders are a feature built into most modern EHR systems. Unlike registries, they operate on a patient-by-patient basis. Reminders help assure that diabetic patients get an annual hemoglobin a1c determination to measure their level of control if the practice has set that as a clinical practice guideline. With the increasing use of the Internet and mobile apps by patients it is predictable that reminders will, and certainly should, extend beyond things that must be done in the office to those that the patient can do to improve their outcomes. The reminder alerts could, and probably should, also go out to the patient in parallel with going to their provider. Personal health records and patient portals provide an obvious tool for doing this.

Reduced Malpractice: There is at least one study that suggests that providers using an EHR have a significantly reduced chance of being sued for malpractice. [9]. There are other studies that suggest that poorly designed EHR systems can produce new forms of clinical errors. [10] One of these errors is failure to notice abnormal results, a problem which may often be the result of poor user interface design. One study suggests an interesting solution – also send abnormal results to the patient. [11] Again personal health records and patient portals provide an obvious vehicle for doing this.

Ongoing Challenges

Despite decades of effort there are at least three key challenges to successful implementation of electronic health records if success is defined to include increased provider productivity and improved quality of care. These are the optimal way to collect data from providers, how to use information technology to improve workflow and process and how best to visualize clinical data to support providers and patients in achieving the best results.

Collecting the Data: Efficiently collecting clinical data from providers and properly coding it is a very difficult problem. The human body is extremely complex. It consists of many parts that are involved in many processes. It is subject to many disorders and malfunctions. As a result, SNOMED CT, the *subset* of SNOMED for electronic health records, has some 311,000 concepts connected by some 1,360,000 links or relationships. How can a busy physician with limited time be expected to accurately navigate something this complex for *every clinical concept* in *each* patient's chart? Obviously, they cannot. This problem was essentially not resolvable in real clinical practice until recently, in large part because computers weren't powerful enough to help. As a result most electronic charting was done either by inputting free text via typing or dictation or by using templates – essentially paper check off forms transferred into a computer. Today these are still, by far, the most common methods for collecting the subjective and objective clinical data obtained from patient interviews and physical examinations. The majority of commercial electronic health record systems use these techniques but there are innovative approaches that take advantage of the power of modern, yet still relatively inexpensive, computers.

M*Modal began in 1998 when a group of three PhD students (Michael Finke, Detlef Koll and Juergen Fritsch) from Carnegie Mellon University's highly ranked School of Computer Science spun voice recognition technology they had been working on into the commercial space by forming Interactive Systems. In 2001 the company was renamed M*Modal and the focus was narrowed to healthcare. It was acquired by MedQuist in 2012 and the entire company took the M*Modal name. It now offers a suite of web services under the name M*Modal Fluency. Specific examples include Fluency Direct (to speech-enable EHRs), Fluency for Imaging (radiology-focused reporting solution), Fluency Mobile (iPad & iPhone based clinical documentation), Fluency for Transcription (traditional back-end clinical documentation service based on human editing), and Fluency for Coding (billing coding workflow with predictive code generation from narrative text).

The technology had for years been very widely used by medical transcription services around the globe. The benefit to the services was that most of the transcription was done automatically so expensive human labor was only needed to correct what the computer got wrong (it tells the humans what it's not certain of) or cannot transcribe at all (it also points those cases out).

Every instance of use goes back to the company's servers which observe the corrections humans make and use that knowledge to further train the system which, over time, gets better even with various speaking styles, languages and dialects. It can now recognize text sufficiently well to put it into the proper section of a note so that, for example, the chief complaint go into that part of the note while the physical exam, assessment and plan go into their respective parts.

If that weren't remarkable enough, in many instances clinical concepts are located in the text and are coded into structured medical terminology such as SNOMED CT and into various coding systems for medications and into ICD, CPT

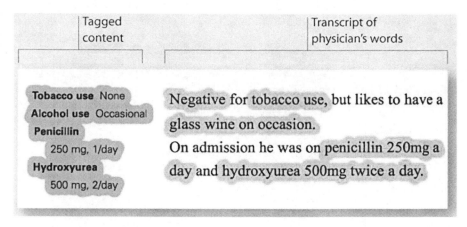

Tagged content	Transcript of physician's words
Tobacco use None	Negative for tobacco use, but likes to have a
Alcohol use Occasional	glass wine on occasion.
Penicillin	
250 mg, 1/day	On admission he was on penicillin 250mg a
Hydroxyurea	day and hydroxyurea 500mg twice a day.
500 mg, 2/day	

Fig. 4.1 M*Modal Recognizes Clinical Concepts in Free Text and Codes them into SNOMED

and LOINC as shown in Fig. 4.1. Here again the system has been trained over time as humans corrected coding mistakes or manually coded those things the computer could not code. The specific accuracy levels are highly dependent on (a) noise levels, (b) medical specialty, (c) amount of similar data previously seen, and (d) the subset of SNOMED codes of interest (e.g. allergies,, diseases, symptoms, procedures). Very specific clinical concepts, such as smoking history, that are normally expressed in one of a few possible ways can be more accurately identified than concepts that can have a large number of possible expressions, such as the patient's problem. High levels of accuracy are possible. For example, the company says it has 97- 100% speech understanding accuracy for radiologists dictating on high quality microphones in a quiet image reading room.

However, the overall accuracy is sufficient that some clients of the company use the technology to code *already digital* text information. They submit it from their system over the Internet to the Fluency for Coding service that identifies the clinical concepts and puts them into the appropriate structured nomenclature, most typically SNOMED CT. Some software is installed locally so that this process works better when there is suboptimal Internet connectivity.

When I first visited the company in 2008 I asked why the technology was not integrated into EMR systems. Back then the company didn't feel it was robust enough. Today, it apparently is, because quite a few EMRs now have M*Modal technology "built in". Again, in all such cases, it is still a web service so the central system continues to learn and further develop from all users.

So voice recognition seems to have arrived as a practical method of collecting and structuring clinical data. To see that in action we'll next look at a leading EMR from a company near my base in Atlanta, and, so far as I know, the first to integrate M*Modal with an EMR.

Greenway Medical Technologies was, according to its web site, founded in 1998 by nearly 100 physicians, clinicians, practice administrators, hospital executives and community leaders with the goal of developing a long-term solution to

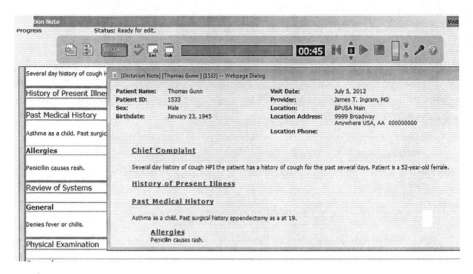

Fig. 4.2 Integration of Speech Recognition into Clinical Documentation

rising healthcare costs, medical errors and decreasing patient safety. Its EHR is called PrimeSUITE®. Fig. 4.2 shows the integration of M*Modal's speech recognition (the speech controls are at the top) into its documentation process. In this example, the physician first imported the past medical history from the patient's face sheet into the new note and then dictated the chief complaint and the history of present illness. M*Modal software recognized what information belongs in those two sections of the chart and placed them accordingly.

There are numerous other places where dictation can go directly into structured forms such as the patient's cover sheet. Dictation process management is also automated so that the resulting text is routed to an internal or external resource for verification and the correction of any mistakes. PrimeSUITE isn't yet converting text to structured clinical concepts but Greenway says that this is their next step.

Integrated Workflow and Process Management: I've repeatedly touched on integrated workflow and process management as an important issue for actually increasing provider productivity through automation. As discussed earlier, the approach is commonplace in manufacturing, retailing and other industries. Finding good examples of this thinking in electronic medical record systems isn't as easy as it should be. Here are two companies that had it among their founding principles.

Medical Informatics Engineering (MIE) was founded in Fort Wayne, IN by Doug Horner in 1995 as a health information exchange including a clinical repository mostly for lab data. This was at the very beginning of the Internet and it is remarkable that the company was web-based from the outset and even provided the needed network connectivity to their clients' offices. Over a series of years their offering evolved into an EHR starting with high speed digital storage and management of transcribed documents. The next phase was to replace paper charts using scanning integrated with bar code technology so the system would understand the contents of each scanned document, technology Doug had previously developed for banking. They began with dermatology, providers who were used to dictating and transcription. Because of its image management, the service allowed them to more compactly have their dictation and diagrams in one place. In these dermatology practices MIE claims to have eliminated paper charts while reducing the number of transcriptionists from 6 to 2 by increasing their productivity.

In 1998 MIE introduced WebChart (which may well have been the first web-based EMR) and their "Minimally Invasive EMR™" around 2000. Doug feels that physicians are and should be "cognitive not clerical". The system "learns" each doctor's practice patterns and, over time, can predict what they are going to input and fills it in for them, a concept that is now widely used in the system. These learned concepts are not problem specific. Instead the system answers questions based on the patient's history and the most common questions for each chief complaint. To give a simple example, in a case typically requiring antibiotic therapy, the drug the physician has most often used in the past for similar cases would appear first on their list of choices. These preferences (e.g. each physician's approach) are built into a "medical library" allowing nurses to switch libraries as they rotate among physicians. MIE provides some interesting case studies on its web site. [12]

Today MIE has around 3000 physician users across the US and around the world. The company also offers a fully integrated personal health record called NoMoreClipboard. Partially as a result of offering both capabilities, it is used extensively in occupational health clinics for major employers who typically use both the EMR and PHR. To give one example of the integration, the EMR evaluates each patient's risk of developing particular chronic diseases, such as diabetes or hypertension, and tells the EHR what questions each patient should answer in the PHR to further evaluate that risk and monitor their progression toward that disease or their success in helping to avoid it.

Praxis was founded by Richard Low, a UCLA/Yale educated physician, who first trained in surgery and did emergency medicine before shifting to internal medicine. He recalls attending a seminar given by a physician/lawyer and first realizing how important medical documentation is. He later found out that the "average physician spends 2.5 hours per day doing paperwork, that's 8.5 years of his career." He examined clinical records and determined that "no two doctors chart the same". His dream was to develop something that would save doctors time while allowing them to maintain their individual approach to charting. He started Praxis in his native Argentina in 1989 with $15,000 of his own money which, he says, went a great deal further there than it would have in the US. Praxis was introduced in 1993 and since its second product release in 1998, has grown as a profitable company with no outside financing. The company is now based in Marina Del Rey, CA.

Ironically the way Praxis makes documentation more efficient for physicians is itself not easy to understand. At its core is the notion of a "clinical concept". Praxis does not define concepts in a standardized way as SNOMED does. Rather they consider a concept an indivisible clinical unit *in the view of each individual physician*. In essence a concept is a basic element of the way the physician thinks about medicine.

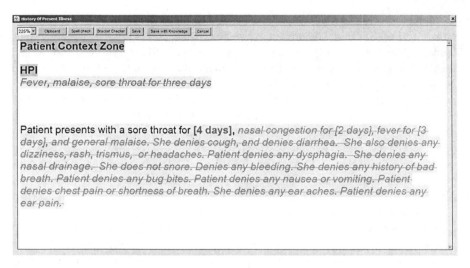

Fig. 4.3 Physicians Using Praxis Select the Most Appropriate Clinical Concepts for Each Patient from Choices that Derive from their Most Similar Prior Cases.

Based on this idea the company developed what it calls a "concept processor". The computer science term for this is an artificial neural network (ANN). An ANN is an advanced computing approach used to model complex relationships between inputs and outputs or to find patterns in data. A bank, for example, might use an ANN to find people who are more likely to be submitting fraudulent credit card charges based on patterns that might not be obvious at all to a person looking at the data, in part because of its massive scale. The technology is also being applied in healthcare to look for fraudulent claims.

The basic idea behind Praxis is that physicians develop a method of going from inputs – such as the history, physical exam and lab results – to outputs such as a diagnosis and treatment plan. Praxis says that its concept processor "learns" how each individual physician does this for the problems they see and uses that knowledge to save the physician time on subsequent visits by essentially anticipating what the physician will likely do and document. The system starts as a "blank slate" in each practice but, over time, it gets better and better at finding the encounter closest to the current one. After around 50 iterations of a particular problem the system is well trained and, according to the company, can accurately find the closest matching or even "identical" prior encounter. Based on that it brings up the clinical concepts the physician has used in the past for similar patients, as illustrated in Fig. 4.3. By doing this the system saves the physician time and also serves to provide clinical reminders, reducing the chance that something will be overlooked or forgotten. Praxis has, laudably in my view, avoided the temptation to automatically document for the physician who must specifically decide what to chart for each patient from the list of concepts presented. The physician can, of course, add more or edit, as appropriate for each case.

Documentation flow in Praxis is quite different than in traditional charting. It normally does not begin with the chief complaint – the patient's own typically vague statement of their problem – as physicians are trained to do. This is because the chief complaint will not provide sufficient specificity for the concept processor to find the best prior case. Physicians using Praxis are trained to first input the most clinically specific "input" (a "clinical finding") they can. This allows the concept processor to more accurately find the identical or best match to the patient being seen. Physicians can group subsets of an overall problem, such as acute pharyngitis (sore throat), according to whatever clinical divisions make sense to them. This further assists in getting to the best possible matching case and its associated clinical concepts. Physicians can post their own personal approach to clinical concepts so, for example, a family physician can import the approach used by an expert neurologist to evaluate headache.

Praxis is available as a hosted service (the company recommends an iPad as the end user device) or as a licensed client-server software program. The company says it has around 3,000 clients with its largest user community being family physicians.

Visualizing the Data: Today, computing is essentially ubiquitous in all fields of endeavor. Across virtually all of those domains our ability to collect and aggregate data is well ahead of our capability to analyze and visualize it effectively. In fact, visualization is now an accepted branch of computer science. It hasn't received enough attention in health informatics which is unfortunate and, I think, likely to change.

Some of the visualization issues in health informatics can be illustrated with the story of a group of my students who entered a challenge to visualize the data in a CCD. Their visualizations were intended to support a busy physician on call for his group who is faced with an unfamiliar patient.[14] Our three teams each decided that a particular aspect of visualization was most important to a busy clinician.

One team emphasized rapid access to any part of the data from any other part. They created a "dial menu" very much like a clock face except that each section was part of the chart – medications, lab results, problem list and so on. The clinician could just point to any section and the information stored in it would pop-up. Clicking on any section provided more detail about the data stored in it.

A second team emphasized configurability of the data presentation. The clinician could control what sections of the data would appear and where they would be located on the screen. It was very easy to move them around, as needed. This approach was very similar to the user configurable "My Whatever" pages so common on the web.

The third team emphasized clinical relationships. The clinician could point to any problem on the patient's list and only the data relevant to that problem would appear. This team won the competition but I was allowed to watch the judges, many

---

[14] The CCD was the one posted on the Internet by Dr. John Halamka that we referred to in the last chapter. [23]

Interventions	MPR ⬍	Conditions	Observations △
2 Spironolactone 50 mg po qday	100%	Congestive Heart Failure	Weight 175
8 Carvedilol 25 mg bid	80%		SBP
6 Hydrochlorothiazide 25 mg po qday	30%	Hypertension	K+
2 Lisinopril 40 mg po qhs	75%		Creat Nebeker
0 Terazosin 5 mg po qhs	80%	Benign Protatic Hypertorphy	Nocturia 1
3 Simvastatin 40 mg po qhs	90%	Coronary Artery Disease	Angina 1.5
na Aspirin 162.5 mg po qday	80%		
3 Glipizide 10 mg po qday	100%	Diabetes Mellitus II	HbgA1c 4
		Depression	PHQ9 5

Fig. 4.4 Visualization of the Interventions and Observations that Relate to a Specific Clinical Condition

of whom were physicians, deliberate and it was clear they would have liked a visualization tool that provided all three capabilities. I would bet that most clinicians agree with the judges but no EHRs yet provide all these capabilities, although many do provide some of the user configurability that team two offered.

People are starting to focus on visualization. A major 2009 report by several committees of the National Research Council reviewed the current state of clinical health informatics and developed a roadmap for the future. One of its key conclusions was that today's systems tend "to squeeze all cognitive support for the clinician through the lens of healthcare transactions and the related raw data, without an underlying representation of a conceptual model for the patient showing how data fit together and which are important or unimportant. As a result, an understanding of the patient can be lost amidst all the data, all the tests, and all the monitoring equipment." [14] I urge readers with a serious interest in cognitive support of providers and patients to read the entire report.

Improved data visualization is a key strategy to implement this recommendation. Implementing it will likely require novel underlying data representations that more clearly mirror the thought processes of healthcare providers. It might also require the development of new systems (sometimes called "middleware") to make the needed data connections. Dr. Jonathan Nebeker, Lead, iEHR Presentation Layer at Veterans Health Administration, presented an interesting proposed user interface based on this idea at the 2012 HIMSS conference (Fig. 4.4).

A lot remains to be done but it is encouraging that visualization of clinical data in ways that can help providers and their patients make more informed decisions now seems to be a topic that is attracting increasing attention.

References

1. Consensus Report (1999) To Err is Human: Building a Safer Health System, National Academies Press http://www.iom.edu/Reports/1999/To-Err-is-Human-Building-A-Safer-Health-System. aspx Accessed 19 July, 2012
2. Classen D *et al* (2011) 'Global Trigger Tool' Shows That Adverse Events In Hospitals May Be Ten Times Greater Than Previously Measured. Health Aff 30:4 581–589

3. http://www.ahrq.gov/consumer/20tips.htm Accessed 19 July, 2012
4. Bleich S (2005) Medical Errors: Five Years After the IOM Report http://www.commonwealth-fund.org/usr_doc/830_Bleich_errors.pdf Accessed 19 July, 2012
5. DesRoches CM *et al* (2008) Electronic Health Records in Ambulatory Care— A National Survey of Physicians. N Engl J Med 359:50–60
6. Jacobs L (2009) Interview with Lawrence Weed, MD—The Father of the Problem-Oriented Medical Record Looks Ahead. Perm J. 13(3):84–9
7. http://well.blogs.nytimes.com/2009/04/02/the-ideology-of-health-care/ Accessed 19 July, 2012
8. Committee on Quality of Healthcare in America (2001) Crossing the Quality Chasm: A New Health System for the 21st Century. The National Academies Press
9. Quinn MA, Kats AM, Kleinman K, Bates DW, Simon SR (2012) The Relationship Between Electronic Health Records and Malpractice Claims. Arch Intern Med. http://archinte.jamanet-work.com/article.aspx?articleid=1203517 Accessed 19 July, 2012
10. Yackel TR and Embi PJ (2010) Unintended errors with EHR-based result management: a case series. J Am Med Inform Assoc. 17(1): 104–107.
11. Cram P, Rosenthal GE *et al* (2005) Failure to recognize and act on abnormal test results: the case of screening bone densitometry. Jt Comm J Qual Patient Saf 31(2):90–7
12. http://www.mieweb.com/solutions/webchart-ehr-case-studies/ Accessed 19 July, 2012
13. http://services.bidmc.org/geekdoctor/johnhalamkaccddocument.xml Accessed 19 July, 2012
14. Stead WW and Lin HS (2009) Computational Technology for Effective Healthcare: Immediate Steps and Strategic Directions, National Research Council http://www.nap.edu/catalog.php?record_id=12572 Accessed 19 July, 2012

Chapter 5
Patient-Centered Care

In this chapter we'll look at some new health informatics tools designed to overcome the challenges of chronic disease management and supporting prevention and wellness in community-based healthcare. Traditionally a provider is focused on each patient, as they physically see them. That is how they were trained. In most circumstances that is what is required to get paid. Is should be no surprise that most electronic medical records reflect this "one patient at a time" view of care.

As we've seen, success in managing chronic disease requires a new model emphasizing "patient-centered care" with continued patient interaction and observation between office visits. While it goes under several names, such as the Chronic Care Model, the Patient-Centered Medical Home and others, they all recognize that, to achieve success, the patient and their providers as a team must manage their health and their chronic medical problems on a continuous basis. Adoption of any of these models requires informatics tools designed to support this new approach.

Medicare's Accountable Care Organizations and similar "outcome-based" reimbursement systems now being offered by the major private insurers provide the economic incentives for this approach to care. In this chapter we will look at the contemporary informatics tools available to implement them.

In Chapter 3 we discussed the long time issue of interoperability among diverse health informatics systems. Historically the focus was on hospitals and health systems who sought to bring together data from many – often more than 100 – diverse and specialized systems so that they could have an integrated view of their administrative and financial status and, more recently, so that clinicians working in their facilities could have an integrated clinical view of their patients.

A proactive, patient-centered view of wellness and prevention and the management of chronic disease places new emphasis on solving this long time problem so that:

A group of geographically dispersed providers can work together to better manage the complex chronic disease patients who, according to the Anderson and Horvath study we cited earlier [1], may typically receive that care from around 14 offices per year.

That same group of providers can proactively manage a contract with an employer or insurance company based on their success as a group in achieving certain defined quality metrics (a financial arrangement often termed "pay-for-performance").

M.L. Braunstein, *Health Informatics in the Cloud*, SpringerBriefs in Computer Science, DOI 10.1007/978-1-4614-5629-2_5, © The Author(s) 2013

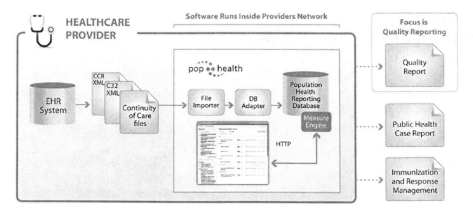

Fig. 5.1 popHealth Collects Quality Metrics without Moving PHI Outside of the Providers' Control

That same group of providers can proactively manage both their care quality and its cost to earn the maximum share of the reduced costs that Medicare, or a private insurer, would rebate to them under an ACO or similar outcome-based payment model.

We will now look at some examples of the health informatics tools for patient-centered care. I cannot promise that they are the best examples or the best for any particular provider practice. My purpose in discussing them is to give a sense of what can be done and how it is done given contemporary health informatics technologies and the mixed landscape of electronic health records that exists in most communities.

popHealth is an open source quality measurement system funded by ONC and developed by the Mitre Corporation. It runs over Laika, an open source EHR testing framework intended to analyze and report on the interoperability capabilities of EHR systems as a part of the EMR certification process. The technology approach is similar to hQuery, another ONC funded open source effort that automates a more generalized set of distributed queries across diverse EHRs for purposes such as clinical research. We'll look at hQuery in more detail in Chapter 7. popHealth captures summary clinical data in one of the standard formats from healthcare providers' EHRs.

Figure 5.1 shows how this works. Certified EHRs produce standard clinical summary files that are imported into popHealth software that is running on the providers' systems. This is a really key concept in popHealth. PHI never leaves the providers' control, greatly simplifying HIPAA issues and alleviating other concerns about how the data might be used.

Once it has extracted abstract data at the provider site for reporting purposes and sent it to the central system, popHealth streamlines the automated generation of summary quality measure reports on the providers' aggregate patient population. In Fig. 5.2 data from 500 patients has been aggregated from a hypothetical group of 10 providers who could be using different EHRs.

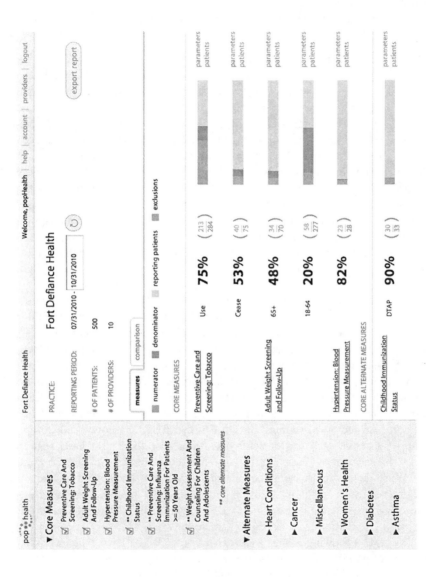

Fig. 5.2 Data Aggregated by popHealth from 500 Patients from 10 Provider Locations is Used to Report on Various Quality Metrics Such as Routine Weight, Smoking and Blood Pressure Screening

This is a typical scenario when a physician network has contracted to provide care under a pay-for-performance approach. Common quality metrics such as tobacco cessation, adult obesity, hypertension screening and childhood immunization status are collected, aggregated and reported in a very simple, easy to understand format.

The system can also provide more focused and detailed analysis at the provider or the patient level.

Medicity is based in part in Atlanta which has one of the largest clusters of health informatics companies in the US. When I first came to Georgia Tech I made it a personal goal to try to identify and become familiar with the most innovative Atlanta-based health informatics companies, particularly with respect to chronic disease management and patient-centered care. One of the first companies I "discovered" was Novo Innovations. One of its co-founders, Robert Connelly, was even a Georgia Tech graduate (the other was Alok Mathur). They became interested in the problem of interoperability while working for Atlanta-based HBOC (now McKesson Provider Technologies), the largest health informatics company in the country. There they developed an early physician portal, a system to give an integrated view of care to community based providers around a hospital or a hospital-based health system. Such a system would typically consist of a hospital and associated provider practices that might be owned by the hospital but, in those days, would typically be independent and would have their own information systems that, back then, would usually not include an EMR.

As is often the case in large companies, they got an idea for a novel interoperability solution and, finding little interest on the part of their employer, left to start their own company. The idea is a bit technical but it is based on "intelligent agents", software that can reside on the same server as an EHR or other clinical system (a laboratory system, for example) and is sufficiently "aware" of that system that it can observe its data flows (often in HL7 specified formats). The best way to explain what happens next is to give a highly simplified example. Dr. Smith has ordered some blood chemistries for her patient, Mrs. Jones. The agent running on the laboratory system and the agent running on Dr. Smith's EHR can communicate and cooperate. As a result, each knows who Mrs. Jones is in their associated system (remember, she probably will have different identifying numbers in each of these systems). When the agent observing the laboratory system's data flows sees a result for a test ordered by Dr. Smith it "grabs" it and sends it, along with some information identifying the patient, to the agent in Dr. Smith's office. That agent figures out whose result it is and puts it into the right place in her EHR.

If you've been following along since earlier, you'll recognize that this is an example both of interoperability – two diverse systems sharing data – and process re-engineering – something once done manually now being automated, saving time, expense and potentially reducing errors. The agents are "intelligent" with respect to the system they are associated with. As a result, they are automating previously manual processes. Unlike the much simpler DIRECT approach to information exchange, people are not guiding the agents to perform each instance where data should be exchanged. In the example given, all laboratory tests ordered by Dr. Smith would end up in the appropriate charts with no further manual effort on the part of Dr. Smith or her staff.

In addition to this process automation, the grid is also an approach to health information exchange. If every clinical system in a health enterprise had the agents installed the resulting "grid" could become an HIE. This was exactly what Novo developed and successfully deployed in a large number of hospitals and health systems. The company claims that the technology is so simple to implement that they could often deploy it without physically visiting their client. Later on the company recognized that the grid could be a "platform" upon which healthcare "apps" could operate and have access to the underlying clinical data. The platform is called iNexx. It's somewhat analogous to the app platforms on a Smartphone which typically do, if the owner of the phone allows it, have access to the underlying data stored on the phone.

Medicity, a major supplier of traditional health information exchange technologies, acquired Novo in 2009 and, in 2010, the combined company was acquired by Aetna, the giant health insurance company. What's going on here? Why would an insurance company want to own advanced tools for health information exchange?

The answer is in large part, the grid, its platform and the apps. Earlier we said that the major private health insurance companies are following Medicare's lead and are offering outcome-based plans structured somewhat like ACOs. This means that if care providers in a network can deliver superior outcomes for less money they get to share in the savings. The details don't matter and are certainly subject to change given how new this is but one problem is clear from our earlier discussion in this chapter – those providers need new tools. Figure 5.3 shows the Aetna Care Collaboration Coordinator, an iNexx app.

As the name implies, this app is designed to facilitate a collaborative and informed approach to care across multiple provider offices *no matter what EMR they have*. Someone in each patient's primary care provider office – this would likely be a care coordinator in a patient-centered practice – indicates what providers are part of this patient's virtual care team. For a patient with multiple chronic diseases this might include their endocrinologist, if they have diabetes, their cardiologist, if they have congestive heart failure, and so on. These providers need not be part of the same practice. To participate, each of these practices must download the free iNexx platform. The download would likely be posted by a Medicity connected health system for providers using its HIE or who are in its provider network. Medicity also contracts to provide the technology to state HIEs so, in that situation, the iNexx platform might be posted for download by any provider connected to the statewide HIE.

Whatever the source, someone is responsible for setting up a local "node" that is, in essence, the master agent through which everything is coordinated. The node automatically finds the iNexx installations in the network to which it is connected creating a local "grid".

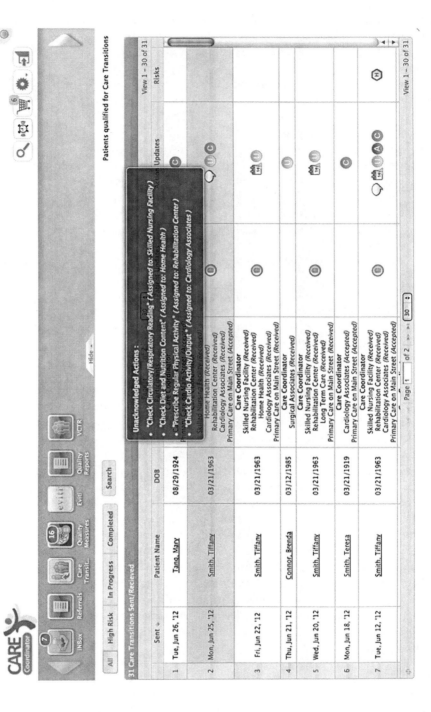

Fig. 5.3 Aetna's Care Collaboration App on the iNexx Platform Tracks the Status of Care Processes and Issues Alerts Against Practice-defined Risk Thresholds

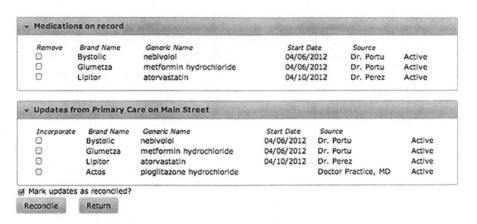

Fig. 5.4 Medication Reconciliation Ensures that Everyone on the Care Team Knows What Everyone Else has Prescribed

So, to review, each practice has the iNexx platform installed. Their local copy is "aware" of what EMR they are using and can integrate with its data flows. It also is "aware" of the local node so it can send and receive data as requested. Figure 5.3 illustrates how the platform can be used. At discharge, a care coordinator can send tasks to various members of the patient's team. These are received at the proper office and the originating office can monitor their status via the icons in the Action Updates column (U – unacknowledged, A – acknowledged, C – Complete or Calendar – Overdue). As shown, clicking on an icon provides the details – in this example, unacknowledged tasks.

This not only creates much needed care coordination but it is an example of process reengineering, something we've discussed repeatedly. Here, an electronic process can replace phone calls, emails, faxes and other more time consuming methods of communicating. Moreover, everything is in one place so things are less likely to slip through the cracks.

The Patient Updates column reports on actions other team members have taken that this office may need to be aware of. An example might be a new medication order. In that case the app can provide a medication reconciliation screen (Fig. 5.4) summarizing what medications the practice has a record of and what medications the grid is aware of. This display can help make sure every office has a clear view of each patient's complete treatment program to help prevent errors and promote patient safety. Medication reconciliation is a Meaningful Use requirement.

Finally, each practice can use the Risks column at the right to display patients meeting their own criteria for being at high risk. It should be obvious at this point that this would be of particular interest to practices under a pay-for-performance or outcome-based reimbursement model. Under such models any extra costs associated with failing to identify these patients early will, at least in part, be borne by the practice. Early detection of increased risk might help avoid expensive complications, or at least delay their development.

Wellcentive was founded in 2005 by a former employee of mine, Mason Beard, and his brother-in-law, Paul Taylor, a practicing physician in Michigan. Paul's organization, a Physician Hospital Organization (PHO) was under a pay-for-performance contract with Blue Cross. A contract like this places demands on the physician group to produce superior clinical outcomes. A PHO by law must be clinically integrated to provide coordinated care, but Paul's organization was attempting to achieve this essentially using spreadsheets. There were a variety of EHRs in use but many practices were documenting on paper.

Mason was working and going to graduate school when they got into a discussion of the problem. Paul felt that their payers, who were only able to look at retrospective claims data, had an inferior view of care to the more timely view that could be assembled from the practices in the PHO if clinical data were aggregated in "real time". Providers also had more detail. For example, the payer might know that a hemoglobin A1c (HbA1c), an important test to follow the clinical status of diabetics, was done but they wouldn't know the value, so it was very hard for them to see if the test was being followed up appropriately. Also, each payer saw their claims but not the claims paid by other payers while the patient's physician could, in theory, have a much more comprehensive view of the care, particularly if data was aggregated from all the practices caring for a patient.

Together they decided to develop a solution. The data they needed was in the systems that supported each practice. The key challenge was getting it and putting it into a useable, more standardized and structured, form. The original proof of concept was web-based and was integrated with a few systems, mainly in clinical laboratories. It also had a generic tool for loading data from other systems. Despite the fact that the tool was primitive by today's standards, the PHO rose significantly in the Blue Cross Physician Group Incentive Program (PGIP) quality rankings. [2]

Today, Wellcentive's data collection and aggregation is most commonly from ANSI 837 claims data, the same data that is sent to the payer, via a direct feed from the practice management system that does billing for the provider office; transfer of LOINC codes from the major lab companies; and HL7 feeds from the local health systems for information about hospitalizations and discharges. Where an HIE is present it is possible to get much of the needed data via an interface to it. The company can accept data in a CCD format via a DIRECT connection but, as of this writing, they say this is just starting to happen.

The Wellcentive Advance suite of products is comprised of four key capabilities called Data Manager, Analytics Manager, Outcomes Manager, and Community Quality Manager and is used by providers in all 50 states. The company says their customers include some of the nation's best known health systems. Data Manager helps these customers map data from their systems to Wellcentive in order to bridge any differences in terminology. The tool takes advantage of the web so customers can collaborate with their business partners to build these maps. For example, a provider network might allow a lab technician in the local hospital to help build a map between the terms used in that laboratory and those used in Wellcentive. The tool also logs and tracks data errors. A common example is a patient not found in one of the systems in the network because of a naming or other difference in key demographic data. These tools are designed to help clients identify and fix data quality issues. Interestingly, this function is increasingly becoming the responsibility of office managers because the tool simplifies what was once thought of as a highly technical function. In most practices, office managers are the people who have historically dealt with coding issues. Analytics Manager allows larger provider networks to incorporate data from loosely affiliated practices even though those practices aren't formally using Wellcentive.

Outcomes Manager is where the data, once collected and aggregated, is used to provide proactive management of wellness and chronic disease in the patient population being cared for by the provider network. The user might be a care coordinator in a PCMH model clinic but many smaller clinics are now outsourcing this function to a new class of independent professionals often referred to as a Care Manager. This allows providers to have access to this needed service without having a full time employee devoted to the task.

The company recently released a fifth capability called Risk Manager. It applies predictive modeling and risk stratification to patient populations in order to find those patients at a high risk for poor clinical and financial outcomes.

Figure 5.5 from Outcomes Manager shows a list of Alerts defined by a practice. For each, the number of qualifying patients (the denominator in the percentage calculation) is shown along with the percentage of patients who don't meet this quality metric. Adjacent to that is a graphical representation of the practice's current quality performance versus their goal for each metric. Red flags indicate metrics below the corresponding goal set by the practice. Practices can define the provider cohort against which these metrics are calculated so, for example, cardiologists could be compared only to other cardiologists. The View Patients link brings up the individual patients who don't meet the goal. The practice then has a number of options including an automated system the company provides to contact each patient to provide reminders, patient education or to request the patients make an appointment. These calls can be customized based on known clinical data so that, for example, a patient with an elevated LDL could be asked to come in to be evaluated for statin therapy. The company also offers a personal health record (PHR). Any patient-entered data is considered unverified. The provider is alerted when it is input and, if they verify the data, it can then be used by the quality management system. Thus, for example, if the patient reports an increased blood pressure that data, once verified, might trigger a "blood pressure not under control" alert for the patient.

Before moving on it's worth reflecting on what we have seen in this chapter. The long time problem of interoperability is being solved, at least within the admittedly limited domains of collecting, aggregating and visualizing clinical quality for specifically defined risk metrics. This is possible because of the new technologies we discussed earlier. It is hard for me to look at these systems and not be optimistic about the future.

The Novo grid is a creature of the Internet. It's possible only because diverse systems across a community can now be bound together into what is effectively a single virtual database. One care coordinator using the iNexx app we examined could, in theory, oversee the management of all the hypertensive or diabetic patients

Fig. 5.5 Wellcentive's Outcomes Manager Tracks Performance Against Contracted Quality Metrics Goals Across an Entire Network of Providers

in an entire community and help assure they don't get out of control between visits to their provider. This is a key goal of all chronic care models and technology is now available to greatly facilitate achieving it. Similarly, popHealth and Wellcentive allow an entire provider network to know each provider in that network and even that each patient of each of those providers is being managed against well defined and accepted quality metrics. This is an essential issue if healthcare quality is to be improved and, ultimately, if costs are to be reduced because problems aren't allowed to get worse over time as a result of important screening or clinical management issues not being routinely addressed.

References

1. Anderson G and Horvath J (2004) The Growing Burden of Chronic Disease in America, Public Health Reports. 119:May–June 2004
2. http://www.bcbsm.com/provider/value_partnerships/pgip/ Accessed 19 July, 2012

Chapter 6
Empowering the Patient

Many years ago I spent an entire day in a crowded hotel room at a world informatics conference in New Orleans. The topic was who owns the digital medical record or, more specifically, how and where it should be stored. This was well in advance of any hope of actually creating such a repository but that didn't keep the conversations from getting quite lively! I clearly remember one thing in particular: the Europeans mostly favored giving each patient a "smartcard" on which their record would be stored and carried around in their possession, while the Americans mostly favored a "Cheyenne mountain" like approach where everyone's records were stored in a massive database.

Today, except in a few places, the US has largely discarded a central approach to electronic record storage in favor of the federated approach in which patient records are stored in part in each of the EHRs of their multiple providers. This creates many issues, not the least of which is unambiguously identifying each patient.

The French, who invented the smartcard, recently required that every citizen over 16 have a "*carte vitale*" health insurance card embedded with a microchip and containing social security insurance details (Fig. 6.1). It does not yet include clinical information, although some pilot studies are being undertaken.

So, while people may disagree on how to do it, everyone agrees that an integrated and complete view of each patient's health record is highly desirable. More recently, with the development of the Internet and mobile technologies, a great deal of discussion has evolved as to whether and how patients might be actively involved in making this happen.

There are at least four platforms for patient engagement. We'll discuss them very roughly in order of increasing involvement on the part of the patient.

M.L. Braunstein, *Health Informatics in the Cloud*, SpringerBriefs in Computer Science, DOI 10.1007/978-1-4614-5629-2_6, © The Author(s) 2013

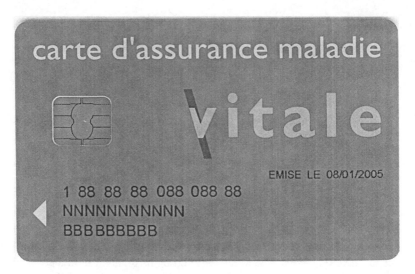

Fig. 6.1 The French National Health Identity Card

Health Web Sites

According to the CDC "research has shown that 74% of all U.S. adults use the Internet, and 61% have used it to look for health or medical information. Additionally, 49% have accessed a website that provides information about a specific medical condition or problem." [1]

I am sure any reader in clinical practice has substantial experience with patients bringing information or even a self diagnosis or treatment proposal from the Internet to an office visit. The issue of how providers incorporate these new patient tools into their practice is far from resolved. [2] [3]

Health web sites can be usefully divided into several groups based on their level of sophistication:

Patient Education: The Mayo Clinic's site [4] is probably the best known example. It is a rich site providing well written monographs describing a huge list of diseases and conditions. Some monographs include a video. Beyond that is information on how conditions are diagnosed and treated at Mayo, available clinical trials, Mayo research into the condition as well as profiles of the researchers in that area and, powerfully, actual patient stories. Not all of these are available for every condition. There are many other well known general patient education sites.[15] There are also numerous sites focused on a specific diagnosis or disease class.

---

[15] familydoctor.org and webmd.com for example.

Patient Search: As mentioned earlier, best practices have yet to be developed for incorporating web tools into clinical practice. The physician concerns in this regard are clearer. They include the lack of reimbursement for email interaction with patients and time wasted with patients who bring in concerns, suggested treatments or diagnoses based on unreliable or inappropriate information.

Personalized search could substantially remedy this. The basic idea is to equip a specialized health search tool with clinical knowledge about the individual using it. This idea is already commonplace – perhaps too commonplace for some of us. Use any of the major search engines and you'll be presented with ads that somehow relate to your interests. What's happening in simple terms is that the search engines are paying attention to what you look for and learning even more detail about you based on what you show interest in by clicking on it. Simply put, if you search for information about cars, then it's far more likely you are in the market to buy one.

Health is a more complex challenge for personalization. People may not know the right terms to use to describe their problem or interest. This is less of a problem with well known and understood items like toaster ovens or cell phones. In addition, many unapproved "cures" and "treatments" are offered and the sites promoting them can be a wealth of misinformation. The Internet in general provides a great deal of misinformation and biased or inexpert opinions. However, it is far less problematic if people buy the wrong coffee maker than if they decide they have some rare, life threatening disease or, if they do have a serious illness, become enamored of a bogus remedy that won't cure it and may even do them harm.

A solution may be linking some form of search to trusted and reliable information about the patient. We'll discuss the approaches to that later in this chapter, but they typically involve some sort of personal health record that is populated with data from the patient, from health claims or from the patient's EHR.

Patient Communities: In the past few years the Internet has morphed from a place where people primarily consume information to one where they are actively involved in contributing it. This "social networking" is arguably the primary use of the Internet today. [5] Whether or not you personally participate, you almost certainly have family members, friends and colleagues that do.

PatientsLikeMe® may be the most sophisticated health social networking site. The company was co-founded in 2004 by three MIT engineers: brothers Benjamin and James Heywood and longtime friend Jeff Cole. Five years earlier, their brother and friend, Stephen Heywood, was diagnosed with ALS (Lou Gehrig's disease) at the age of 29. The Heywood family soon began searching the world for ideas that would extend and improve Stephen's life. They envisioned an environment for sharing and collecting data, typically on innovative treatments for incurable disease. To accomplish this, social networking was built on a research platform. Getting patients engaged in aggregated clinical research was their primary mission.

The site is free to patients and accepts no advertising but it is not a non-profit business. The objective is to gather data from patients about their illness experience and make that available in aggregated form to organizations that are interested in particular populations of patients. Examples would be pharmaceutical companies or companies with early stage products that want to learn from patients that have the condition they seek to treat. For example, a pharmaceutical company might partner with the site to create a portal for engaging organ transplant recipients, a site within the site, where it can talk to patients and learn from them while at the same time considering the aggregated data. At present the site has 1500 conditions. Prior to April 2011 there were 20.

To create a clinically relevant research platform, PatientsLikeMe uses structured surveys to collect patient-reported data. Novel treatment, symptom and condition data enter the "User Voice dashboard" where it is reviewed and curated to assure data integrity. They receive around seventy-five "user voice" entries per day. Some may already be in the system. For example, there could be a spelling difference, or the patient could have entered two concepts together, such as "pain and depression". These are split so the patient can monitor each separately and each can be aggregated for research purposes.

All clinical data is coded in the background using standardized terminologies. Symptoms and side effects are coded into SNOMED-CT and MedDRA, a medical terminology used to classify adverse events associated with the use of biopharmaceuticals and other medical products. Diagnoses are coded into ICD-10, the next generation of this coding system that is not yet widely used in the US. Despite this high degree of coding, as much as possible the "patient voice" is maintained.

PatientsLikeMe points out that patients self-manage around 90% of their care. As shown in Fig. 6.2, the site helps patients put their conditions in context, organize the status of symptoms, treatments and side effects and prepare themselves for a clinician encounter through the use of a clinician visit sheet. They try to help patients answer the question "given my status what's the best outcome I can hope to achieve and how do I get there"? They offer patients connections to other similar patients and patient communities

PatientsLikeMe is perhaps best known for a dramatic research study initiated by the patients themselves. After a report from Italy suggested that Lithium might slow the progression of their disease, a group of patients with amyotrophic lateral sclerosis (ALS) decided to experiment on their own with lithium carbonate treatment. They came to the site and said, "we're using lithium and need support to find the effects." In 12 months using the tools on the site patients showed that Lithium had no effect on their disease progression. [6] Nothing I know of more dramatically illustrates the potential for patient participation in their own health and in clinical research through making data more accessible and easier to share, aggregate and analyze.

Patient Portals: This is a concept that preceded the Personal Health Record (PHR) and is still around today. McKesson Provider Technologies, whose RelayHealth division is a leader in this space, has a patent for an electronic method of communication between healthcare providers and patients involving personalized web pages for doctors and their patients. They may have been the first to offer such a service.

The basic idea of any patient portal is a web page that facilitates communication between patients and their health providers. Potential functions include secure

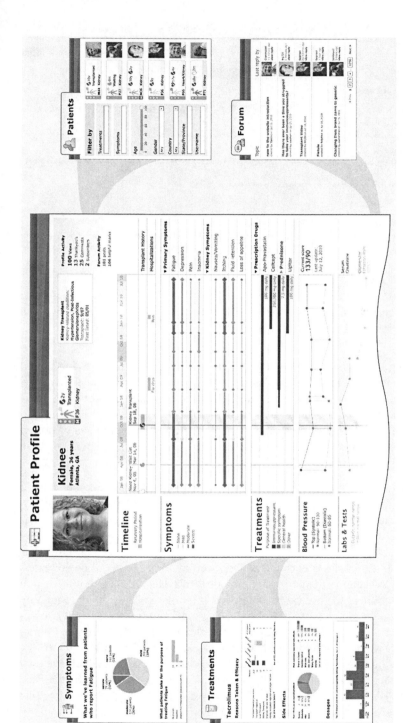

Fig. 6.2 PatientsLikeMe Helps Patients Put Their Symptoms and Treatments in Context and Find Similar Patients and Forums Focused on Their Condition.

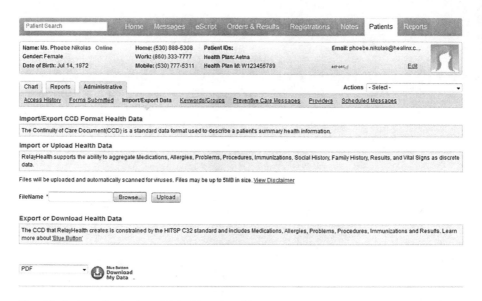

Fig. 6.3 Patients Can Upload Clinical Data in a CCD or the Blue Button Format into RelayHealth from their Provider's EHR

email, making appointments and viewing test results. In general patients don't input their own clinical data into a portal. Some portals now include the capability for a patient to upload their clinical data in the CCD format from their provider's EHR into their PHR. Alternately, some PHRs allow veterans to use the Blue Button [7] to upload their clinical data from the VA's VistA EHR. The Blue Button can be posted by any web site that wants to offer veterans this same capability. Both of these options are illustrated in Fig. 6.3.

RelayHealth was founded in 1999 as Healinx by Assaf Morag, another HBOC (now McKesson Provider Technologies) employee to leave to start a company. Assaf first got me thinking about the role of the Internet in linking patients with their care providers. The name was later changed to RelayHealth and it was subsequently acquired by McKesson Provider Technologies. Today their patient portal serves over 2,000,000 activated patients and is interfaced to all of the major health enterprise systems. A health system typically provides RelayHealth's health information exchange capabilities for use by its employed providers or those that commonly refer patients to the health system. RelayHealth's platform enables clinical integration of data (HL7, CCD, etc.) between systems, and also includes a frontend portal for those users who do not have an EMR. RelayHealth's platform also supports the VA's Blue Button format. In 2011 RelayHealth won the Blue Button Challenge (and $50,000 which it donated to charity) by being the first vendor to support the Blue Button. If an EMR vendor cannot send or receive a CCD, they can use the Blue Button format to share data, even for non-veterans. (Fig. 6.3)

The platform is optimized to build a longitudinal patient record by integrating with clinical inpatient systems such as the billing system, the emergency department system, the inpatient EHR, the laboratory system, the radiology system, and the transcription system via HL7 and CCD standards. Ambulatory EHRs can use either the CCD format or HL7 to integrate with RelayHealth. For coordination of care, support for DIRECT is planned by year-end 2012. The company also has plans to support the new Transitions of Care (TOC) Consolidated CDA format, a version of the CCD with contents designed for situations where patients move from one care venue to another. An example would be discharge from a hospital to a rehabilitation facility after surgery.

The end result is that patients get an integrated inpatient/outpatient longitudinal patient record as well as tools to manage their care. They can also get a total family record -- parents and children's health records in one place. Patients can contribute most of their data but RelayHealth does not yet support uploads from devices such as glucometers or digital scales.

Appointment requests can be made through the portal. These requests are routed to the staff members within a practice that are trained to interface with the RelayHealth portal in order to receive them. Patients can also request prescription renewals and refills through the system. All such transactions are routed to pharmacies through SureScripts, the nationwide network that interconnects them. [8] ePrescribing is a key Meaningful Use requirement so this can be an important feature for provider practices.

The system provides patient-to-provider and provider-to-provider secure messaging as well as management of sending orders and receiving their results. The patient's primary care physician gets automatic notification of any emergency department visits, an important feature to help assure continuity of care.

To support all this functionality RelayHealth provides a cross organizational master patient index (XMPI) and does extensive terminology mapping to and from its base nomenclature of SNOMED for clinical problems, ICD-9 for diagnoses and Medi-Span[16] for medications.

Personal Health Records (PHR): While the Internet and mobile devices have made patient journaling of health information far more feasible, this, like most other "innovations" in health informatics, is not a new idea. At least one 1978 paper is commonly cited in a discussion of the history of the concept. [9] Today, PHRs are an active topic of discussion, research and development. [10] [11]

A PHR is a patient-maintained record of health and health related information. Decades ago, before home glucometry was technically and economically feasible, physicians might ask their diabetic patients to maintain a journal of their urine glucose measurements taken using a colometric chemical strip test. The concept of

---

[16] MediSpan is one of the commercial providers of extensive medication databases. Other providers include FirstDataBank, Micromedex, Gold Standard, and Multum.

web-based PHRs gained enormous attention in October, 2007 when Microsoft launched HealthVault. [12] Google followed them in 2008 but withdrew from the market in 2011.

In early 2007 Aetna launched a pilot PHR based on the extensive claims data they already had for the employees of their clients. This is a very appealing concept since it removes from the patient much of the burden of correctly entering their own health data. On the other hand, as with all claims data, the amount of clinical detail is less than ideal. It can be known, for example, that a test was done but the results will not be in a claim. The company later introduced SmartSource[SM] technology that personalized health searches based on the information in a person's PHR. [13]

In 2006, America's Health Insurance Plans (AHIP) and the Blue Cross and Blue Shield Association (BCBSA) worked together to identify the core information to include in PHRs, and also developed and pilot tested draft standards to enable consumers to transfer PHR data when they change coverage. [14] This eventually led to the development of an HL7 Plan-to-Plan standard that was published in May, 2011. [15]

HealthVault was funded and incubated within Microsoft starting in 2005 by Peter Neupert and Sean Nolan who met when they were both at drugstore.com during the great Internet boom of the 1990s. Both had family situations that caused them to be interested in healthcare so they decided to do a health startup. Peter talked to current Microsoft CEO, Steve Ballmer, while the two of them were jogging, and they became convinced that doing something significant in a slow moving industry like healthcare required a large corporate umbrella. They also felt that the new business could benefit by leveraging Microsoft's technology relationship with virtually every hospital.

I interviewed Sean, now a Distinguished Engineer at Microsoft, and he says he learned over the ensuing years that interoperability and innovation in healthcare were harder and took longer than he had expected. Today, based on the many factors we've been discussing, he feels they are finally in the right place at the right time, something he expressed by saying that "patients as a hub of information sharing are going to be a key part of our healthcare system".

So far HealthVault has been most successfully introduced to people when they are having a life event such as a baby, getting a new medical diagnosis, having a medical emergency or having a parent getting older and needing help. At that point a key advisor such as a physician can best introduce people to PHR technology. HealthVault agrees with others that employers also make sense as a point to introduce PHRs, but has not focused on them yet.

Sean believes that over the next two years there will be sufficient saturation of interoperability that the market will start to take off. HealthVault has very successfully implemented an app platform and, today, they have 300 of them along with 80 medical devices that utilize it. Sean emphasized that their API is platform agnostic (it even works with iPhones). Through the API a developer could ask the HealthVault for "all this patient's blood pressures" or "all those over systolic over 120". Consent for use of their data, along with all other stored information, is entirely managed by the patient.

Both the American Heart Association (AHA) and the American Diabetes Association (ADA) have used the HealthVault API as part of tools they have created for patient management of diseases within their respective domains. AHA's Heart360 [16] allows patients to track and manage their heart related health data, access additional information and resources on how to be heart healthy, and share their results with their provider. A separate app for providers allows them to see how their patients with a heart condition are doing. Again, the HealthVault system manages consent to assure that patients are always in full control of access to their data.

The Telcare® Blood Glucose Meter is another interesting example of the PHR as a health app platform. It uploads results directly to HealthVault without the need for a Smartphone. The patient, their caregivers and their health providers can all access the data with the patient controlling who is in their "network" and can view their information. [17]

There are other important providers of PHRs. The Dossia Consortium, a not-for-profit association of major employers, was formed in 2006 and provides an open-source, secure, PHR platform supporting apps for consumer, patients and providers. [18] An interesting example in public health was developed with the New York City Department of Health and Mental Hygiene (DOHMH) and consists of two components: 1) a dashboard (external to the PHR) that provides volunteer workers with graphical population and individual level tracking and reporting, intervention, communication and contextual education materials; and 2) a Dossia PHR app that tracks a hypertension initiative. Other PHR apps provide health risk assessment, medication management and other capabilities along an integrated health record that includes data from medical devices (wireless blood pressure cuff and scale).

MediKeeper was founded in 2003 and launched its PHR in 2004. Today it also supports PHR apps and provides other software for risk assessment as well as a patient portal. [19]

Patient Apps

In January, 2007 Apple® introduced the iPhone® and the idea that virtually anyone could create relatively simple programs ("apps") and efficiently sell them through an online store without having to deal with the details of software distribution and online e-commerce. Today the iPhone and Google's Android™ are the two most popular Smartphones and there are over 500,000 apps in each of their stores. A site that tracks mobile technology publishes a "Consumer Health Apps for Apple's iPhone" report that it says lists over 13,000 apps. [20]

As would be expected, the patient health apps vary enormously in sophistication, functionality and the degree to which they are directly involved in patient care. A search of the Apple app store for "blood pressure" finds 86 apps. Most allow patients to manually enter their readings so they can graph and track them and even send them by email to their physicians. Patients are not covered by HIPAA so they can even do this using regular email if they wish. More sophisticated apps such as the iHealth™ Blood Pressure Dock actually collect the data, in this case by connecting to the company's FDA cleared wrist blood pressure measurement device. This company also offers a digital scale that communicates wirelessly with an iPhone via Bluetooth®. [21] Data collection by Smartphones may potentially even include an ECG. At least one company has announced a technology in which the ECG leads are embedded in a special Smartphone case. This approach has not yet been FDA cleared. [22] Given the sophistication of these apps, it should not be surprising that the FDA is considering what its involvement in regulating mobile health applications should be and it is currently soliciting public comment before issuing regulations. [23]

There are examples of the phone being used as a health measurement device. A group at Georgia Tech Research Institute is developing iTrem, an app that measures patient's tremors using the accelerometers built into Smartphones. [24] SkinScan™ uses the Smartphone's camera to take pictures of lesions of concern to the patient and even analyzes them to advise the patient if they need to see a dermatologist. [25]

Other apps are offered for use by clinicians. One assists in interpreting ECGs. [26] Apps are being offered as devices for use in hospitals and even in critical care. At least one company is marketing an FDA-cleared platform that allows waveforms from patient monitoring systems to be accessed by their clinician via a Smartphone or tablet computer. [27]

This technology will become more embedded in healthcare delivery over time, particularly as the apps implement the data representation and transport standards that are increasingly in use by EHR systems. They also introduce obvious new problems in securing and insuring the privacy of PHI and in verifying the trust necessary to know that health data is being sent where it is intended to go.

Before leaving health apps it is worth noting that there is some, but not yet a lot, of evidence that mobile phones, and specifically their SMS text messaging capability, can be used to change patient behavior, a critical issue in prevention and management of chronic disease. A 2009 literature review of 14 studies that met the inclusion criteria found that behavior change interventions delivered by SMS can have positive short-term outcome but suggested that more and better research was needed. [28] Preliminary results of an ongoing literature review here at Georgia Tech found 21 studies published in 27 papers looking at the use of SMS to improve diabetes management and indicates that there is not yet a consensus about what works. [29] One recent and widely publicized study suggests that SMS text messaging can be cost effectively used to achieve at least short term reductions in smoking. [30] Similar results were found by a group of Georgia Tech researchers for management of pediatric asthma patients. [31]

I am aware of no studies in peer reviewed journals on the impact of actual mobile apps on patient behavior or clinical outcomes. A significant challenge for the "app" model is understanding what in the design of an application makes it effective, particularly in terms of patient engagement. Health communication research and psychology research, such as social cognitive theory, have long sought to understand what influences human behavior, and more to the point, what influences a person to change their behavior. Health apps offer the possibility to answer long standing questions by making it possible to monitor what information a person pays attention to and how they communicate with care providers and people in their social network. Health apps also suggest new questions, such as how an online game can catalyze learning about a health condition and motivate healthy behavior. For example the MAHI app for diabetes management increased patients' internal locus of control (an individual's belief that he can influence future health outcomes) and their willingness to experiment with healthy eating alternatives [32]. However, currently there are wide gulfs between the design of new health apps and understanding what makes them effective. This is clearly an area in need of more study.

Home Telehealth

Patients must manage chronic disease in their homes so it is not surprising that technology for their use at home has been an active area for research and development for many years. These technologies divide into several sub areas.

Subjective data about symptoms or status that patients enter into a portal or PHR can be of some value to their care providers.

Significantly more value can be obtained from objective data such as weight, blood pressure or blood glucose. It is becoming more common for patients at home to obtain their own physiologic measurements.

Technology could provide ongoing advice and assistance to patients in managing their diet, exercise and medications. With relatively inexpensive equipment and a high speed Internet connection a care coordinator could make virtual home visits when the data from the patient indicates one might be appropriate.

Research at Georgia Tech suggests that, in time, it might be possible that technology in the home could monitor patient behavior to help detect issues like a decline in clinical status for a patient with congestive heart failure based on changes in their movement patterns or even a failure to take prescribed medications. This field is called "behavior imaging", essentially sensing and understanding patient behavior remotely through various technologies. The technology is already being provided commercially for use in the assessment and treatment of behavioral disorders such as autism. [33]

These functions, taken as a whole, comprise the still developing field of home telemedicine. One of the first people to think deeply about the field was Steve Kaufman who founded HealthTech Services in 1988 where he developed a device called HANC, a physically large and quite expensive home care nursing robot and assistant to aid a broad range of home care patients in achieving what he calls "supported independence".

Technology with some of these functions has gotten far more compact and inexpensive but financial incentives in healthcare have not, at least up until now, facilitated its use. In many ways the problem is similar to provider use of email. It makes perfect sense but it won't happen if providers only get paid for physical visits. The advent of outcome-based payment could change this dynamic. If providers are interested in achieving the best outcomes and if technology in the home is shown to more than pay for itself by helping achieve them, then it would be logical for providers to see that they are provided even if they have to pay for them.

Despite the reimbursement issue, there are numerous commercial home telehealth products on the market. The simplest and least expensive deliver a single physiologic measurement such as blood pressure. They may be Bluetooth® enabled so that the data can go to a cell phone and, from there, to a web site. Often this data flow is a service provided for a monthly fee by the device maker. While this business model is attractive to companies since recurring revenue is far more lucrative and, hence, more valuable than one time device purchases, it risks creating a series of "walled gardens", each of which has its own narrow view of the patient.

There are initiatives and offerings designed to avoid this happening. The Continua™ Health Alliance was created in 2006 by a group of technology, medical device and healthcare delivery organizations and now has 240 members. [34] The goal is to create standards for interoperable home telehealth devices and services in three major categories: chronic disease management, aging independently, and health & physical fitness.

Even without such standards, exporting telehealth data from the home to a PHR can integrate it with data from other devices and with the rest of the patient's clinical record. Qualcomm's Health Management division offers their own approach to this integration. [35] Their 2net™ Hub Platform includes two components. The first is a small hub device that plugs into an electrical outlet and provides single point collection of wireless health data in the home. It supports the Bluetooth®, Bluetooth Low Energy, WiFi and ANT+ local area radio protocols. It is also Continua™ certified. The second component is a cloud-based service for aggregation and analysis of the data. The data can be sent from there to EHRs and other systems operated by providers or other organizations interested in the patient's status. It can also be sent to the patient's PHR. According to the company the system was designed and engineered to meet all HIPAA requirements.

References

1. Cohen RA and Adams PF (2011) Use of the Internet for Health Information: United States, 2009. NCHS Data Brief no 66
2. Forkner-Dunn J (2003) Internet-based Patient Self-care: The Next Generation of Healthcare Delivery. J Med Internet Res. 5(2): e8
3. Gerber BS and Eiser AR (2001) The Patient-Physician Relationship in the Internet Age: Future Prospects and the Research Agenda. J Med Internet Res 3(2):e15
4. http://www.mayoclinic.org/patienteducation-rst/ Accessed 19 July, 2012
5. http://www.jeffbullas.com/2011/09/02/20-stunning-social-media-statistics/
6. Wick P, Vaughan TE, Massagli MP and Heywood J (2011) Accelerated clinical discovery using self-reported patient data collected online and a patient-matching algorithm. Nat Biotechnol. 29(5):411-4.
7. http://www.va.gov/bluebutton/ Accessed 19 July, 2012
8. http://www.surescripts.com/ Accessed 19 July, 2012
9. Computerisation of personal health records (1978) Health Visit. Jun;51(6):227
10. Kaelber DC et al (2008) A Research Agenda for Personal Health Records (PHRs). J Am Med Inform Assoc Nov-Dec; 15(6): 729–736

11. Schnipper JL *et al* (2012) Effects of an online personal health record on medication accuracy and safety: a cluster-randomized trial. J Am Med Inform Assoc doi:10.1136
12. http://techcrunch.com/2007/10/04/microsoft-beats-google-to-online-health-records-with-healthvault/ Accessed 19 July, 2012
13. http://www.aetna.com/showcase/smartsource/ Accessed 19 July, 2012
14. http://www.ama-assn.org/amednews/2007/01/01/bisb0101.htm Accessed 19 July, 2012
15. http://www.hl7.org/documentcenter/public_temp_8910ECF5-1C23-BA17-0C61DD 4BEF7E40C5/pressreleases/HL7_PRESS_20110502.pdf Accessed 23 September, 2012
16. https://www.heart360.org/ Accessed 19 July, 2012
17. http://telcare.com/ Accessed 19 July, 2012
18. http://www.dossia.org/ Accessed 19 July, 2012
19. http://www.medikeeper.com/ Accessed 19 July, 2012
20. http://mobihealthnews.com/research/consumer-health-apps-for-apples-iphone/ Accessed 19 July, 2012
21. http://www.ihealth99.com/ Accessed 19 July, 2012
22. http://alivecor.com/ Accessed 19 July, 2012
23. http://www.fda.gov/medicaldevices/productsandmedicalprocedures/ucm255978.htm Accessed 19 July, 2012
24. http://eosl.gtri.gatech.edu/Capabilities/LandmarcResearchCenter/LandmarcProjects/iTrem/ tabid/798/Default.aspx Accessed 19 July, 2012
25. http://skinscan.com/ Accessed 19 July, 2012
26. http://itunes.apple.com/us/app/ecg-interpreter-calipers-treatment/id422853571?mt=8 Accessed 19 July, 2012
27. http://www.airstriptech.com/ Accessed 19 July, 2012
28. Fjeldsoe BS, Marshall AL and Miller YD (2009) Behavior change interventions delivered by mobile telephone short-message service. Am J Prev Med, 36(2):65–173
29. Han Y, Abowd GD, Arriaga, RI (2012) A Review of Diabetes Management Systems on Mobile Phones. Manuscript in preparation
30. Wells J *et al* (2012) Cost-effectiveness Analysis of a Mobile Phone SMS Text-based Smoking Cessation Intervention. UTMJ 89(3):160-165
31. Tae-Jung Y, *et al* (2012) Using SMS to provide continuous assessment and improve health outcomes for children with asthma. Proceedings of the 2nd ACM SIGHIT International Health Informatics Symposium (IHI '12). ACM, NY, NY 621-630.
32. Mamykina L, Mynatt E, Davidson P and Greenblatt D (2008) MAHI: investigation of social scaffolding for reflective thinking in diabetes management. Proceeding of the twenty-sixth annual SIGCHI conference on Human factors in computing systems ACM 477-486.
33. http://www.behaviorimaging.com/ Accessed 19 July, 2012
34. http://www.continuaalliance.org/ Accessed 19 July, 2012
35. http://www.qualcomm.com/solutions/healthcare Accessed 19 July, 2012

Chapter 7
Increasing Knowledge

Going all the way back to Larry Weed it has been a goal of health informatics that clinical data from electronic records could be aggregated, analyzed and visualized in ways that would contribute to our understanding of the natural course of disease, the clinical effectiveness and safety of the treatments we employ once they are out in the community, more effective understanding and control of public health and other purposes such as finding patients who qualify for clinical trials.

This is much simpler in a centralized model of health information exchange, such as they have in Indiana. Key clinical data is abstracted from all the connected systems and is curated into a more standardized and structured form that is ideal for all the purposes just listed. However, the US is moving strongly away from this model in favor of a federated approach for both economic and political reasons. In such a model each provider's data is stored only in their EHR. There are also hundreds of EHR products that providers can implement to qualify for Meaningful Use and they don't represent data in a consistent way.

Despite the increased difficulty of aggregating data, good arguments can be made in favor of the federated approach:

Each health organization maintains their own HIPAA-mandated contractual control of their PHI.

Local content experts have the strongest relationship with and best understanding of their own data.

It is easier to manage consent locally where direct contact with the patient is easiest and trust is greatest.

Federation reduces the scale of data breaches and concerns about exposing data to competitors.

In addition to the federation of the data here in the US we will have hundreds of regional and statewide health information exchanges operated by health systems that may have competitive reasons for being reluctant to share their data.

M.L. Braunstein, *Health Informatics in the Cloud*, SpringerBriefs in Computer Science, DOI 10.1007/978-1-4614-5629-2_7, © The Author(s) 2013

Finally, there are some significant technical issues including:

How to express a clear clinical question in a way that disparate computer systems can all properly interpret it
   Developing a standard for expressing clinical terms and concepts
   Overcoming the lack of consistency among providers in data coding

In summary, the challenge is how to collect, aggregate and meaningfully analyze clinical data from such a complex set of systems and technologies in an environment with no real standards for data representation.

This question is important enough that it's been given a name: distributed population queries. It was the subject of a series of web meetings sponsored by ONC in the summer of 2011 and is an initiative of the Standards and Interoperability collaborative community of volunteers from the public and private sectors. [1] This group has created a set of proposed Query Health standards. The details are quite technical but basically they sit on top of the already agreed to standards for data representation (e.g. coding systems like SNOMED) and packaging into documents (e.g. CDA).

Query Health involves two new standards. The first is referred to as the "envelope" and it contains the query and any associated policy requirements. This must include information needed for systems at the receiving location to make sure their internal security and privacy guidelines are not violated by the query.

The second new standard is the Query itself. It is expressed in an XML format similar to that already used in CDA documents thus assuring it can be read by virtually any EHR while avoiding the need for an entirely new query standard.

There are at least three existing open source implementations of distributed query PopMedNet [2], i2b2 [3] and hQuery [4].

PopMedNet™ was developed for Harvard Pilgrim Healthcare Institute and the Harvard Medical School, Department of Population Medicine. It consists of two components, the Portal and the DataMart Client. The system assumes a group of entities have created a collaborative network for shared research. There is a single Portal for each such network where requests are made and where all system communications, security, and governance policies are managed. Each collaborator on the network has their own local DataMart Client. A collaborator could be a hospital, an individual clinic or any other entity that has stored clinical data. A key goal of this design is that PHI never leaves each collaborator's system. Queries get processed by the DataMart Client and the local system and only the results go back to the Portal.

PopMedNet is being used in the FDA Mini-Sentinel project [5] [6] to assess the safety of already approved drugs, biologics, and devices in actual clinical practice. As of December, 2011 the population being assessed consisted of 126 million patients. An example of its use was the rapid evaluation of cardiac outcomes of patients using drugs for smoking cessation. This was a proof of concept that was not designed to produce useful results but it did work without the need to transfer any PHI over the network.

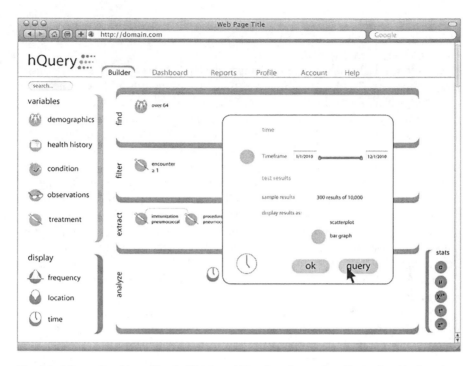

Fig. 7.1 hQuery Provides a Simple Web-based User Interface to Specify the Specific Questions for which Answers are Sought

Informatics for Integrating Biology and the Bedside (i2b2) is an NIH-funded collaborative research project involving many of the major health and technology institutions in Boston. Its core mission includes bringing together routine patient data obtained in clinical care with the genome-wide measurements made of the corresponding patients. This is often expressed as combining genomic data with the phenotypic data to gain a deeper understanding of the impact of genomic alleles (variations).

The i2b2 analog to PopMedNet's Portal is called the i2b2 "Hive". The Hive consists of substitutable and interoperable software components called "Cells" and of a persistent data storage called the Clinical Research Chart. Many of the cells have a user level interface and are grouped in the "Workbench" where users can search the i2b2 terminology, build and store queries with concepts from this terminology, and visualize the resulting data. It has been used with reasonable success at the University of Utah to test the applicability of an asthma exacerbation predication tool developed in Boston on the patient data resident in their institution. [7]

hQuery is an open-source implementation of a framework for distributed query of health data funded by ONC. For ease of implementation and use it emphasizes a simple approach based on current web standards, as shown in Fig. 7.1. Like the other technologies, hQuery provides distributed query capabilities that maintain

PHI behind the provider or HIE firewall while supporting population reporting. hQuery integrates with certified EHR systems by leveraging their ability to generate CCD or CCR patient summaries.

Certify, a health information exchange vendor based in San Jose, CA, has a unique "appliance" called HealthDock™ that, like Medicity's grid, is aware of the EHR with which it is co-located and can facilitate data exchange with it. The technology is claimed to go beyond that and to actually facilitate distributed query of clinical data found in any EHR connected to a Certify HIE via a HealthDock.

While it's not really distributed query in the sense we've been discussing, Greenway Medical Technologies, a major EHR vendor, offers an interesting approach to clinical research across those practices that use its products. Through its PrimeRESEARCH service clinical research organizations (CRO) or other clinical researchers can find patients that match their study criteria from among the 50+ enrolled certified research sites. When a certified research site decides to enroll their patients into a study, the clinical trial can be performed by directly documenting data in the EHR and exporting it back to the CRO. The study can be managed through the CTMS-Clinical Trials Management System within the Greenway application suite.

The Centers for Disease Control and Prevention have recently launched the BioSense 2.0 program, an interesting example of nation-wide cloud-based information aggregation, analysis and visualization of electronic health information from federated systems in emergency departments and urgent care centers. The goal is to track emerging health problems as they evolve. This could potentially include acts of bioterrorism. The development team indicates it has plans to support data collection via both the CONNECT and DIRECT approaches to Health information exchange. [9, 10]

References

 1. http://wiki.siframework.org/Query+Health Accessed 19 July, 2012
 2. http://www.popmednet.org/ Accessed 19 July, 2012
 3. https://www.i2b2.org/ Accessed 19 July, 2012
 4. http://projecthquery.org/ Accessed 19 July, 2012
 5. http://mini-sentinel.org/ Accessed 19 July, 2012
 6. http://www.mini-sentinel.org/work_products/Data_Activities/GroupAdminManual_Mini-Sentinel_v2.2_v1.0x.pdf Accessed 19 July, 2012
 7. Meystre SM, Deshmukh VG and Mitchell J. (2009) A Clinical Use Case to Evaluate the i2b2 Hive: Predicting Asthma Exacerbations, AMIA Annu Symp Proc. 2009; 442–446.
 8. http://projectpophealth.org/ Accessed 19 July, 2012
 9. http://www.cdc.gov/biosense/index.html Accessed 23 September, 2012
10. http://www.facebook.com/#!/CDCBioSenseProgram Accessed 23 September, 2012

Chapter 8
What's Next

Before taking a look at a possible future, let's quickly review where we've been and where we are today.

The core potential benefits of electronic records are to support providers in making correct clinical decisions, to facilitate coordination of care, particularly for chronic disease, and to provide data to improve medical knowledge, our understanding of treatments in a broad patient population and public health. There is also the hope that properly designed and implemented systems will increase efficiency by improving processes and workflows.

How the US delivers healthcare is unique and is best characterized as a "complex adaptive system" in which there are many independent agents, each of whom acts in their own perceived self interest and no one is in charge. This led to a long time impasse in which providers were expected to invest in technology when most of the financial benefits would accrue to payers. This was a major reason why adoption of "fully functional" electronic records that could help achieve the desired benefits was extremely low as recently as 2008. Other impediments were the complexity of the technology and providers' reasonable concerns that they would not select the correct systems nor be able to properly implement them.

In 2001 the Institute of Medicine sounded an alarm. It said clearly that US healthcare was overly expensive, did not produce the desired results in an alarmingly high percentage of cases and was even often unsafe. The IOM recognized the potential role of information technology in solving these problems and soon thereafter called for a new engineered approach to health delivery. During this same period, the federal government became, of necessity, increasingly concerned about rising healthcare costs. In 2004 President Bush proclaimed universal adoption of electronic records as a national priority. In 2009 President Obama used the stimulus to bridge the complex adaptive system and offer payment for adoption if providers used the technology in a "meaningful" way that offered the prospect of reducing health costs while increasing the quality of care, particularly through coordinated care for the chronic diseases which now account for a substantial majority of US health costs.

In parallel Medicare and several of the major private health insurance companies are offering outcome-based contracting for care under which providers are rewarded

M.L. Braunstein, *Health Informatics in the Cloud*, SpringerBriefs in Computer Science, DOI 10.1007/978-1-4614-5629-2_8, © The Author(s) 2013

for producing better outcomes at lower cost. The Medicare ACO pilot studies and the experience at some leading health systems already under an outcome-based business model strongly suggest that health informatics can help achieve the desired results. This means that providers have a further incentive to adopt electronic records and other technologies for improved clinical decision support, care coordination, information exchange, management against quality metrics and patient empowerment. Providers should reasonably be willing to invest in these technologies to the extent that they can improve care outcomes while lowering costs if those reductions exceed the cost of the technology.

This federal investment and these new economic models have had at least two important results so far. The adoption of electronic records capable of Meaningful Use may have now reached 40% of providers and nearly 50% of hospitals. These federal programs are widely known and reported. Less widely appreciated is the impact this investment is having by creating a more favorable environment for investment in entrepreneurial companies, particularly those developing lighter, simpler, less expensive cloud-based systems. It is tempting to say that this is simply the health informatics industry finally adopting the technologies that have already revolutionized other industries. It is equally tempting to say that it's happening now because the needed web, mobile and wireless technologies are now mature and robust enough for use in healthcare. These statements may well both be true but it's hard to imagine the huge burst of entrepreneurial activity we are seeing today if the entrepreneurs could not make a strong case that their innovative products would find a ready market.

So, what's next? First, in the book so far, I've done my best to stick to the facts. What follows is largely my opinion. Please read it in that light.

Dealing with Legacy Systems

The most common objection to the federal deployment effort is that we are baking in a generation of technologically obsolete and not well designed electronic record systems that aren't interoperable and that will therefore collectively become an impediment for achieving the very goals we just listed. It is hard to argue against part of this premise. Many commercial health informatics products are old and were developed using very proprietary technologies. This makes interoperability harder to achieve. Their user interfaces are often poor compared to the best of what is now available. These design shortcomings can contribute to new forms of error. Poor design is also an impediment to efficient and effective training, proper use and the ability to accomplish many of the desired qualitative and efficiency goals. To make matters even worse, the largest vendors have typically been around the longest, have the largest customer bases and revenue streams, so they can afford the largest and most effective marketing and sales efforts and, therefore, tend to dominate the market.

Here's where my old friend and former health informatics consultant, Steve Rushing, comes to the rescue. Steve has a saying for every occasion. By now I've heard them all (many times!) and the one I've heard the most is "Perfect is the enemy of good" (Steve, according to Wikipedia this is commonly attributed to Voltaire's poem, *La Bégueule*). This is a very hard concept for many people to accept. Particularly hard if they are very detail oriented perfectionists, as many engineers and computer scientists tend to be.

So, in this case, what is good enough? The designers of the EHR certification and Meaningful Use programs clearly tried to answer these questions. All certified EHRs must be able to produce a CCD. While the actual information content of a CCD is not tightly defined by certification (e.g. the content is not tightly specified in most cases and data that would ideally be structured may be in free text) this is clearly a large step forward. It means, in essence, that every EHR can present at least key clinical data in a manner can be reasonably well understood and used by outside systems creating, in essence, a virtual distributed database consisting of all deployed and certified EHRs.

This is not just a theoretical possibility. A startup company I advise [17] has succeeded in mining data almost exclusively from CCDs to create a quality metric reporting system that is installed and in use commercially in a number of medical practices. Of course they had to build software that would curate the data into a standard enough form to do it, but that can be done, particularly for the limited dataset needed to satisfy a well defined set of quality metrics. The hope is that the ability to largely avoid custom interfaces will substantially reduce the cost and complexity of implementing and installing such systems.

We have also seen the emergence of DIRECT as a simpler way to think of information exchange. It does not have many, or even most, of the sophisticated privacy or patient indexing characteristics of the central model. Information is not aggregated, curated, standardized and annotated to allow the kind of one click access to an entire distributed patient record found at the VA or in Indianapolis. However, it works and it should be sustainable. In time, just as social networking has grown more technologically sophisticated, so will the use of DIRECT.

Taken together, these changes may have real and substantial ramifications. We have talked about quality metric reporting. In Chapter 7 we looked at systems that are being developed with the expectation that they could query this entire virtual database for clinical research, public health reporting and other important reasons. That is another really big step forward. While things are far from perfect it is reasonable to expect that, in time, the bar will be raised as everyone gets plugged in and more comfortable in this new world of more open data exchange.

Will the underlying EHR systems become more modern, easier to use and simpler to install? One would hope so. However, real reinvention is very difficult within an ongoing business that also has to respond to customer, market and regulatory demands and keep its investors or shareholders happy. Significant innovation most often happens when new entrants come along. They can start with the proverbial

---

[17] Full disclosure, I have a small financial interest in it so I won't specifically mention it here.

clean piece of paper. The barriers to entry are fairly low in the provider EHR market and, indeed, we are seeing many new companies enter it. It's even lower in new markets such as registries and quality reporting. Reinventing hospital information systems would require a tremendous effort requiring a well funded startup company with a sound and probably phased strategy for market entry. If it is going to happen – this is pure speculation – it may well be from new companies created abroad with India and/or China being the most likely sources. I certainly hope the next generation of health enterprise systems is developed here, but it may not be.

App Platforms

Several PHR and even some HIE technology vendors have recognized the potential value that could be created if they make the data they store or have access to available through a standard set of conventions (usually called an API) to app developers. The Harvard SMART platform [1] extends this idea to an EHR developed specifically for this purpose. I see no reason why this idea cannot be implemented by commercial EHR vendors. It is also possible to envision that some standard set of APIs might be developed such that one app can work with most, if not all, compliant EHRs. The pressure to do this would likely have to come from the healthcare industry or the government. It is tempting to wonder if this might also happen, in time, in the large legacy health enterprise information systems.

What's requited is that all involved recognize the potential to view their products as a "database" that could connect to interested users of that data more powerfully and facilely through an "app platform". It is very tempting to draw a parallel to the app platforms and marketplaces that are already *de rigueur* in the Smartphone space but these new health platforms would have significantly greater complexity given the amount of data that could be made available, its complexity and the strict demands for privacy, security and trust. However, data is being liberated in other domains, why not healthcare?

The Future of Home Telehealth

This is an old concept but, for the most part, the underlying technologies have not changed much. Some progress has been made. Scales, blood pressure and other measurement devices now have Bluetooth® which now works well enough that the need for managing wires has been largely eliminated so devices can be placed more conveniently for the patient. The scale, for example, can be placed in its traditional bathroom location. Touch technology is far better and less expensive because touch panels are now so widely used in cars, new tablet computers and other devices. However, for the most part, today's in-home telehealth products are surprisingly similar, both functionally and technologically, to what was offered a decade or more ago.

What might change this? Certainly outcome-based contracting may have a large impact on deployment but what will improve the usability and acceptability of the technology itself? What will lead to greater success in changing patient behaviors?

All current telehealth technologies represent, to one degree or another, an intrusion of "foreign" devices into the home. To an elderly person this can be threatening or intimidating. Suppose the patient's interface to this new technology was through something far more familiar, their TV? People use them on a daily basis. The screens are large enough that even the elderly can easily read them. Digital TVs are really a specialized computer. Most are now capable of being connected to the Internet. Some even provide an "app platform" but the user interfaces tend to be very poor and getting to the apps involves leaving the "TV world" and going into a quite different space that is unfamiliar to the user. What if these limitations were overcome and the app and TV worlds were seamlessly integrated? TIVO has gone some distance down this road, but not very far. If, as is widely rumored, Apple and/or Microsoft introduce TVs would they not go much further? Microsoft has developed a new app layer for Windows 8 that is claimed to work seamlessly across Smartphones, tablet computers and regular PCs. Might the TV be next?

I think this is highly likely, even if Apple and Microsoft do not actually build a TV. Both already offer a device to turn an existing TV into an app platform. Microsoft may be further down that road for health since they have HealthVault and their Windows 8 app platform is said to work with their XBox, a device most people think of as a game console but that is clearly capable of doing more. They also produce a device called Kinect that could potentially allow people to control their TV with gestures. Kinect might also be a future part of in-home behavior imaging. In fact, thanks to a startup called Equiso, we may not have to wait for these giants. They claim to have developed a $69 USB stick that can turn any TV into a SmartTV. [2] For patients at home, could the TV be the long sought gateway to better health?

Understanding and Improving Process

A few health informatics vendors have placed significant emphasis on workflow and process automation and I've profiled some of them. At least one enterprise software solution is also based on process.[18] However, these are the exceptions, and healthcare is not nearly as sophisticated in designing and optimizing clinical processes as some other industries, so much remains to be done.

At Georgia Tech I have been involved in two research efforts directed at bringing novel technologies and approaches to the understanding and optimization of clinical processes. The first of these efforts began at Georgia Tech's Tennenbaum Institute under the leadership of Bill Rouse. The basic idea is to use the modeling and simulation technologies already commonplace in other domains to gain a better

---

[18] http://www.siemenssoarian.com/

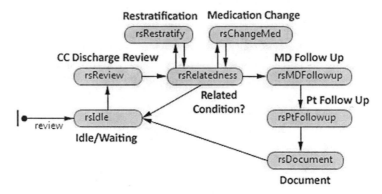

Fig. 8.1 A Clinical Process Model for the PCMH's Follow-up After an Emergency Department Visit or Hospitalization

understanding of existing clinical processes and to provide policy makers with a "what if" tool to explore possible new models. The initial effort successfully modeled the Predictive Health Institute, a joint Emory-Georgia Tech initiative. The model helped show the *future* return on investment due to reduced health costs could more than justify an investment *now* in a program to accomplish those future reductions. [3] Our current effort is directed at modeling patient-centered care. Figure 8.1 shows an example of process representation in this evolving new model. It also illustrates the more structured approach to events, such as an unexpected emergency room visit or hospitalization, in a patient-centered care model.

The second project, just now getting started, seeks to use simulation and other technologies to allow planners to better understand the impact of space design and health IT configuration decisions on the quality and efficiency of care processes. [4]

There are many more exciting possibilities than space allows me to discuss. As I gaze into my crystal ball, at least some of the long deferred dreams of the health informatics community seem to be finally coming true … in large part in the cloud.

As always, we'll have to wait a while to see how it comes out in the end.

References

1. http://www.smartplatforms.org/
2. http://www.kickstarter.com/projects/2028163448/equiso-smart-tv-turn-any-tv-into-a-smart-tv
3. Park H, Clear T, Rouse WB, Basole RC, Braunstein ML, Brigham K, and Cunningham L (In Press) Multi-Level Simulation of Health Delivery Enterprises: A Prospective Tool for Policy, Strategy, Planning and Management. INFORMS Service Science
4. http://www.simtigrate.gatech.edu/

Glossary of Terms and Acronyms

ACO (Accountable Care Organization) MEDICARE's outcomes-based contracting approach

ARRA (American Recovery and Reconstruction Act) the Obama administration's 2009 economic stimulus bill

CCD (Continuity of Care Document) an XML-based patient summary based on the CDA architecture

CCR (Continuity of Care Record) an XML-based patient summary format that preceded CDA

CDA (Clinical Document Architecture) an XML-based markup standard intended to specify the encoding, structure and semantics of clinical documents

CMS (Centers for Medicare & Medicaid Services) the component of the Department of Health and Human Services that administers the Medicare and Medicaid programs

CONNECT ONC supported open source software for managing the centralized model of health information exchange

CPT (Current Procedural Terminology) the American Medical Association's standard for coding medical procedures

DIRECT a set of ONC supported standards for secure exchange of health information using secure email

EHR (Electronic Health Record) a stakeholder wide electronic record of a patient's complete health situation

EMPI an enterprise master patient index

EMR (Electronic Medical Record) an electronic record used by a licensed professional care provider

Health System a network of providers that are affiliated for the more integrated delivery of care

HIE (Health Information Exchange) the sharing of digital health information by the various stakeholders involved, including the patient

HIPAA (Health Insurance Portability and Accountability Act of 1996) legislation to secure health insurance for employees changing jobs and simplify administration with electronic transactions. It also defines the rules concerning patient privacy and security for PHI

HISP (Health ISP) a component of DIRECT that provides a provider directory, secure email addresses and public-key infrastructure (PKI)

HIT (Health Information Technology) the set of tools needed to facilitate electronic documentation and management of healthcare delivery

HITSP (Healthcare Information Technology Standards Panel) a public/private partnership to promote interoperability through standards

HL7 (Health Level 7) a not-for-profit global organization to establish standards for interoperability

ICD (International Classification of Disease) the World Health Organization's almost universally used standard codes for diagnoses. The current version is ICD-10 but ICD-9 is used in most US institutions. The conversion target, set by CMS, is currently October 1, 2013

IHTSDO (International Health Terminology Standard Development Organisation) the multinational organization that maintains SNOMED

LOINC (Logical Observation Identifiers Names and Codes) the Regenstrief Institute's standard for laboratory and clinical observations

MedDRA (Medical Dictionary for Regulatory Activities) the International Conference on Harmonisation's classification of adverse event information associated with the use of biopharmaceuticals and other medical products

MPI (Master Patient Index) software to provide correct matching of patients across multiple software systems, typically within a health enterprise

MUMPS (Massachusetts General Utility Multi-Programming System) an integrated programming language and file management system designed in the late 1960's for medical data processing

NDC (National Drug Codes) the Food and Drug Administration's numbering system for all medications commercially available in the US

ONC (Office of the National Coordinator for Health Information Technology) the agency created in 2004 within the Department of Health and Human Services to promote the deployment of HIT in the US

PCMH (Patient-Centered Medical Home) a team based healthcare delivery model often particularly focused on the management of chronic disease

PHI (Protected Health Information) any health or health related information that can be related back to a specific patient. PHI is subject to HIPAA regulations.

Read Codes a hierarchical clinical terminology system used in General Practice in the United Kingdom

SNOMED (Standard Nomenclature of Medicine) a comprehensive, hierarchical terminology system for all domains of health care and medicine

SNOMED-CT (Standard Nomenclature of Medicine) SNOMED subset for the electronic health record

ToC (Transition of Care Initiative) the effort to develop a standard electronic clinical summary for transitions of care from one venue to another

TPO HIPAA exception for providers, insurance companies and other health-care entities to exchange information necessary for Treatment, Payment or Operations of healthcare businesses

VistA (Veterans Health Information Systems and Technology Architecture) the Veteran's Administration's system wide, MUMPS based health information infrastructure

XML (Xtensible Markup Language) a widely used standard for machine and human readable electronic documents

XMPI a cross organizational master patient index capable of dealing with many unaffiliated hospitals and health systems

Resources

If this book has piqued your interest and you want to explore the topics presented in more depth, I recommend reading these publications in approximately the order they are listed. The Weed book is not available on-line and is expensive to purchase, so try you local medical library:

Medical records, medical education, and patient care; The problem-oriented record as a basic tool. Press of Case Western Reserve University, Distributed by Year Book Medical Publishers, Chicago 1970

Crossing the Quality Chasm: A New Health System for the 21st Century http://www.nap.edu/html/quality_chasm/reportbrief.pdf

The Rise In Spending Among Medicare Beneficiaries: The Role of Chronic Disease Prevalence and Changes in Treatment Intensity http://content.healthaffairs.org/content/25/5/w378.full

The Growing Burden of Chronic Disease in America http://www.ncbi.nlm.nih.gov/pmc/articles/PMC1497638/pdf/15158105.pdf

Healthcare as a Complex Adaptive System http://www.ti.gatech.edu/docs/Rouse%20NAEBridge2008%20HealthcareComplexity.pdf

Electronic Health Records in Ambulatory Care — A National Survey of Physicians http://www.nejm.org/doi/full/10.1056/NEJMsa0802005

Building ACOs and Outcome Based Contracting in the Commercial Market: Provider and Payor Perspectives http://www.ebglaw.com/files/47636_Hastings-Lutes-Friedberg-THINC-ACO-Report.pdf

The Indiana Network For Patient Care: A Working Local Health Information Infrastructure http://content.healthaffairs.org/content/24/5/1214.full

Six Questions to Consider about Merging a CCD http://www.hl7standards.com/blog/2012/01/24/merging-a-ccd/

M.L. Braunstein, *Health Informatics in the Cloud*, SpringerBriefs in Computer Science,   95
DOI 10.1007/978-1-4614-5629-2, © The Author(s) 2013

Computational Technology for Effective Healthcare: Immediate Steps and Strategic Directions, National Research Council http://www.nap.edu/catalog.php?record_id=12572

Providers seeking advice on selecting an EHR would do well to refer to these sources. Some are advertiser or vendor supported, so keep that in mind.

The American Academy of Family Physicians has been actively endorsing EHR adoption for years. Their *Center for Health* informatics runs a free web site to help providers select one (some parts require AAFP membership): http://www.centerforhit.org/online/chit/home.html

These sites provide EHR rankings from provider surveys:

AAFP EHR User Satisfaction Survey (requires membership): https://secure.aafp.org/login/

KLAS EMR Ratings (providers must register but it's free): http://www.klasresearch.com/EMR_Software

Black Book Rankings (by specialty, reports must be purchased): http://www.blackbookrankings.com/healthcare/rankings-ambulatory-physician-emr.php

To keep up with health informatics here are a few – there are a lot more of them – well respected and, I think, reliable resources:

These resources are usually non-technical:

iHealthBeat by the California HealthCare Foundation (I read this daily): http://www.ihealthbeat.org/
HITECHAnswers has EHR buying guides (ads): http://www.hitechanswers.net/

If you are more technically inclined:
John Halamka's blog: http://geekdoctor.blogspot.com/
Gartner's Wes Rishel's blog: http://blogs.gartner.com/wes_rishel/
http://www.emrandhipaa.com/
HISTalk blog by an anonymous hospital CIO (ads): http://histalk2.com/

If you have even more time, this site is an index to health informatics blogs:

HITSphere by Shahid N. Shah, "The Health informatics Guy" (ads): http://hitsphere.com/

If you want to get actively involved in developing health informatics interoperability standards ("real world" providers are involved):

The Standards and Interoperability (S&I) Framework: http://www.siframework.org/

About the Author

After MIT – where I may have spent more time with the Cambridge-based characters in *Hackers: Heroes of the Computer Revolution* by Steven Levy then I did on my course work – I entered the Medical University of South Carolina (MUSC) in Charleston near my home town, interested in software for medicine.

Early on I was fortunate to fall under the spell of the late Dr. Hiram Curry, a short, heavy-set violin maker, distinguished Harvard-trained neurologist and a former family doctor, who was creating the first full academic medical school department for the then nascent field of family medicine. I can still vividly recall the strong sunlight angled steeply down from a high window in his impossibly crowded office in the hospital late that Friday afternoon when I first met him. After hearing me discuss my interest in developing an electronic medical record, he gave me Dr. Larry Weed's then recently published book (*Medical records, medical education, and patient care: The problem-oriented record as a basic tool*). A book, as it turned out, that would change my life. In the final chapter he linked organized, structured medical records with computerization. I read it twice over the weekend; returned to Dr. Curry's office early Monday morning; navigated through his overly protective secretary; and announced I wanted to develop a problem-oriented electronic record for his new clinic. This quickly led to a meeting with the dean, the late Dr. J.F.A. McManus, a huge bear of a man and a pathologist who had done a lot of early work on mitochondrial bodies. I think my MIT degree – very unusual for a medical student back then – must have worked magic, because he gave me $18,000 which we later leveraged into a substantial federal grant to develop one of the first fully functional ambulatory electronic medical record systems. [1] [2]

That early clinic had many, if not most, of the characteristics we now associate with a Patient Centered Medical Home (PCMH). In keeping with a key component of the PCMH – a team approach to care – records and a common problem list were shared by nurses, medical, dental residents and pharmacy students, practitioners of social work and other related disciplines. We even experimented with population health management and quality reporting tools. Dr. Weed's prescience in seeing the role electronic medical records could play in ensuring the quality of care and as a basis for research was the inspiration for much of what we did.

M.L. Braunstein, *Health Informatics in the Cloud*, SpringerBriefs in Computer Science, 97
DOI 10.1007/978-1-4614-5629-2, © The Author(s) 2013

Bolstered by that success we tried to use the core patient record component to create what would now be called a health information exchange (HIE) in rural Hampton County, SC. Despite the enthusiasm and support of the late visionary physician, Dr. Harrison Peeples, we couldn't get the other medical offices to use it, even for free. In retrospect, that was my first exposure to the realities of physician adoption of information technology. The problem was, in retrospect, the lack of incentives to share information, a problem that persists to this day.

I later started a successful company based on the pharmacy component of the family medicine record and spent the next 30 years running mostly clinically oriented healthcare software businesses before I joined Georgia Tech in 2007. Yes, we did do billing, but I never had any real passion for it. I was always more focused on the role of information technology to help the practitioner – whether a physician, nurse or pharmacist – or, more recently, the patient, make care safer, more effective and more efficient.

1. Braunstein ML, (1976) The Computer in a Family Practice Center: A 'Public' Utility for Patient Care, Teaching and Research. *Medical Data Processing*, PP 761-68, Laudet M, Anderson J, and Bego F, Editors. London, Taylor and Francis
2. Policy Implications of Medical Information Systems (1977) Office of Technology Assessment. http://www.princeton.edu/~ota/disk3/1977/7708/7708.PDF Accessed 19 July 2012

CPSIA information can be obtained at www.ICGtesting.com
Printed in the USA
LVOW080225211212

312722LV00002B/26/P